BARBRA STREISAND

WOMEN of ACHIEVEMENT

BARBRA STREISAND

Rita Pappas

CHELSEA HOUSE PUBLISHERS
PHILADELPHIA

Frontis: A woman of record: Barbra Streisand is listed in the *1999 Guinness Book of World Records* for the "Longest Career on U.S. Top 20." Her first hit single, "People," came in 1964; 32 years and seven months later the Top 20 would include her single "I Finally Found Someone."

Cover photo: Kevin Mazur/London Features International, Ltd.

Chelsea House Publishers
EDITOR IN CHIEF Stephen Reginald
PRODUCTION MANAGER Pamela Loos
ART DIRECTOR Sara Davis
DIRECTOR OF PHOTOGRAPHY Judy L. Hasday
MANAGING EDITOR James D. Gallagher
SENIOR PRODUCTION EDITOR J. Christopher Higgins

Staff for **Barbra Streisand**
SENIOR EDITOR LeeAnne Gelletly
CONTRIBUTING EDITOR Judy L. Hasday
ASSOCIATE ART DIRECTOR Takeshi Takahashi
DESIGNER Emiliano Begnardi
PICTURE RESEARCHER Patricia Burns
COVER DESIGNER Emiliano Begnardi

The Chelsea House World Wide Web address is
http://www.chelseahouse.com

First Printing
1 3 5 7 9 8 6 4 2

Library of Congress Cataloging-in-Publication Data

Pappas, Rita.
Barbra Streisand/Rita Pappas.
   p. cm. — (Women of achievement)
Discography: p.
Filmography: p.
Includes bibliographical references (p.) and index.
ISBN 0-7910-5285-0 — ISBN 0-7910-5286-9 (pbk.)
1. Streisand, Barbra—Juvenile literature. 2. Singers—United States—Biography—Juvenile literature. [1. Streisand, Barbra. 2. Singers. 3. Actors and actresses. 4. Women—Biography.] I. Series.

ML3930.S88 S54 2000
782.42164'092—dc21
[B]   00-029438

CONTENTS

WOMEN of ACHIEVEMENT

Jane Addams
SOCIAL WORKER

Madeleine Albright
STATESWOMAN

Marian Anderson
SINGER

Susan B. Anthony
WOMAN SUFFRAGIST

Clara Barton
AMERICAN RED CROSS FOUNDER

Margaret Bourke–White
PHOTOGRAPHER

Rachel Carson
BIOLOGIST AND AUTHOR

Cher
SINGER AND ACTRESS

Hillary Rodham Clinton
FIRST LADY AND ATTORNEY

Katie Couric
JOURNALIST

Diana, Princess of Wales
HUMANITARIAN

Emily Dickinson
POET

Elizabeth Dole
POLITICIAN

Amelia Earhart
AVIATOR

Gloria Estefan
SINGER

Jodie Foster
ACTRESS AND DIRECTOR

Betty Friedan
FEMINIST

Althea Gibson
TENNIS CHAMPION

Ruth Bader Ginsburg
SUPREME COURT JUSTICE

Helen Hayes
ACTRESS

Katharine Hepburn
ACTRESS

Mahalia Jackson
GOSPEL SINGER

Helen Keller
HUMANITARIAN

**Ann Landers/
Abigail Van Buren**
COLUMNISTS

Barbara McClintock
BIOLOGIST

Margaret Mead
ANTHROPOLOGIST

Edna St. Vincent Millay
POET

Julia Morgan
ARCHITECT

Toni Morrison
AUTHOR

Grandma Moses
PAINTER

Lucretia Mott
WOMAN SUFFRAGIST

Sandra Day O'Connor
SUPREME COURT JUSTICE

Rosie O'Donnell
ENTERTAINER AND COMEDIAN

Georgia O'Keeffe
PAINTER

Eleanor Roosevelt
DIPLOMAT AND HUMANITARIAN

Wilma Rudolph
CHAMPION ATHLETE

Elizabeth Cady Stanton
WOMAN SUFFRAGIST

Harriet Beecher Stowe
AUTHOR AND ABOLITIONIST

Barbra Streisand
ENTERTAINER

Elizabeth Taylor
ACTRESS AND ACTIVIST

Mother Teresa
HUMANITARIAN AND
RELIGIOUS LEADER

Barbara Walters
JOURNALIST

Edith Wharton
AUTHOR

Phillis Wheatley
POET

Oprah Winfrey
ENTERTAINER

Babe Didrikson Zaharias
CHAMPION ATHLETE

"REMEMBER THE LADIES"

MATINA S. HORNER

"Remember the Ladies." That is what Abigail Adams wrote to her husband John, then a delegate to the Continental Congress, as the Founding Fathers met in Philadelphia to form a new nation in March of 1776. "Be more generous and favorable to them than your ancestors. Do not put such unlimited power in the hands of the Husbands. If particular care and attention is not paid to the Ladies," Abigail Adams warned, "we are determined to foment a Rebellion, and will not hold ourselves bound by any Laws in which we have no voice, or Representation."

The words of Abigail Adams, one of the earliest American advocates of women's rights, were prophetic. Because when we have not "remembered the ladies," they have, by their words and deeds, reminded us so forcefully of the omission that we cannot fail to remember them. For the history of American women is as interesting and varied as the history of our nation as a whole. American women have played an integral part in founding, settling, and building our country. Some we remember as remarkable women who—against great odds—achieved distinction in the public arena: Anne Hutchinson, who in the 17th century became a charismatic religious leader; Phillis Wheatley, an 18th-century black slave who became a poet; Susan B. Anthony, whose name is synonymous with the 19th-century women's rights movement, and who led the struggle to enfranchise women; and in the 20th century, Amelia Earhart, the first woman to cross the Atlantic Ocean by air.

These extraordinary women certainly merit our admiration, but other women, "common women," many of them all but forgotten, should also be recognized for their contributions to American thought and culture. Women have been community builders; they have founded schools and formed voluntary associations to help those in need; they have assumed the major responsibility for rearing children, passing on from one generation to the next the values that keep a culture alive. These and innumerable other contributions, once ignored, are now being recognized by scholars, students, and the public. It is exciting and gratifying that a part of our history that was hardly acknowledged a few generations ago is now being studied and brought to light.

In recent decades, the field of women's history has grown from obscurity to a politically controversial splinter movement to academic respectability, in many cases mainstreamed into such traditional disciplines as history, economics, and psychology. Scholars of women, both female and male, have organized research centers at such prestigious institutions as Wellesley College, Stanford University, and the University of California. Other notable centers for women's studies are the Center for the American Woman and Politics at the Eagleton Institute of Politics at Rutgers University; the Henry A. Murray Research Center for the Study of Lives, at Radcliffe College; and the Women's Research and Education Institute, the research arm of the Congressional Caucus on Women's Issues. Other scholars and public figures have established archives and libraries, such as the Schlesinger Library on the History of Women in America, at Radcliffe College, and the Sophia Smith Collection, at Smith College, to collect and preserve the written and tangible legacies of women.

From the initial donation of the Women's Rights Collection in 1943, the Schlesinger Library grew to encompass vast collections documenting the manifold accomplishments of American women. Simultaneously, the women's movement in general and the academic discipline of women's studies in particular also began with a narrow definition and gradually expanded their mandate. Early causes, such as woman suffrage and social reform, abolition, and organized labor were joined by newer concerns, such as the history of women in business and the professions and in politics and government; the study of the family; and social issues such as health policy and education.

Women, as historian Arthur M. Schlesinger, jr., once pointed out, "have constituted the most spectacular casualty of traditional history. They have made up at least half the human race, but you could never tell that by looking at the books historians write." The new breed of historians is remedying that omission. They have written books about immigrant women and about working-class women who struggled for survival in cities and about black women who met the challenges of life in rural areas. They are telling the stories of women who, despite the barriers of tradition and economics, became lawyers and doctors and public figures.

The women's studies movement has also led scholars to question traditional interpretations of their respective disciplines. For example, the study of war has traditionally been an exercise in military and political analysis, an examination of strategies planned and executed by men. But scholars of women's history have pointed out that wars have also been periods of tremendous change and even opportunity for women, because the very absence of men on the home front enabled them to expand their educational, economic, and professional activities and to assume leadership in their homes.

The early scholars of women's history showed a unique brand of courage in choosing to investigate new subjects and take new approaches to old ones. Often, like their subjects, they endured criticism and even ostracism by their academic colleagues. But their efforts have unquestionably been worthwhile, because with the publication of each new study and book another piece of the historical patchwork is sewn into place, revealing an increasingly comprehensive picture of the role of women in our rich and varied history.

Such books on groups of women are essential, but books that focus on the lives of individuals are equally indispensable. Biographies can be inspirational, offering their readers the example of people with vision who have looked outside themselves for their goals and have often struggled against great obstacles to achieve them. Marian Anderson, for instance, had to overcome racial bigotry in order to perfect her art and perform as a concert singer. Isadora Duncan defied the rules of classical dance to find true artistic freedom. Jane Addams had to break down society's notions of the proper role for women in order to create new social situations, notably the settlement house. All of these women had to come to terms both with themselves and with the world in which they lived. Only then could they move ahead as pioneers in their chosen callings.

Biography can inspire not only by adulation but also by realism. It helps us to see not only the qualities in others that we hope to emulate, but also, perhaps, the weaknesses that made them "human." By helping us identify with the subject on a more personal level they help us feel that we, too, can achieve such goals. We read about Eleanor Roosevelt, for instance, who occupied a unique and seemingly enviable position as the wife of the president. Yet we can sympathize with her inner dilemma; an inherently shy woman, she had to force herself to live a most public life in order to use her position to benefit others. We may not be able to imagine ourselves having the immense poetic talent of Emily Dickinson, but from her story we can understand the challenges faced by a creative woman who was expected to fulfill many family responsibilities. And though few of us will ever reach the level of athletic accomplishment displayed by Wilma Rudolph or Babe Zaharias, we can still appreciate their spirit, their overwhelming will to excel.

A biography is a multifaceted lens. It is first of all a magnification, the intimate examination of one particular life. But at the same time, it is a wide-angle lens, informing us about the world in which the subject lived. We come away from reading about one life knowing more about the social, political, and economic fabric of the time. It is for this reason, perhaps, that the great New England essayist Ralph Waldo Emerson wrote in 1841, "There is properly no history: only biography." And it is also why biography, and particularly women's biography, will continue to fascinate writers and readers alike.

Barbra Joan Streisand—at the beginning of an entertainment career that would span several decades.

1

A STAR IS BORN

A few days before Thanksgiving, 1961, a skinny girl carrying a stack of sheet music, a red plastic briefcase, and a bag of turkey sandwiches walked into the St. James Theater in New York. Just 19 years old, she was about to audition for the first time for a Broadway show. Barbra Joan Streisand knew this was an important moment in her life. She had spent the past year and a half singing in small Greenwich Village bars and at the Blue Angel, an uptown club. Earlier that year, she had landed a role in the cast of an off-Broadway revue, *Another Evening with Harry Stoones*, which had just closed after only one performance.

Now Barbra had the chance she had been waiting for ever since she was a schoolgirl in Brooklyn practicing Johnny Mathis songs and listening to her own full, rich voice ringing through the hallways of her apartment house. Manhattan suddenly seemed extremely far away from Brooklyn, and despite Barbra's elation, a wave of terror swept over her. But she decided to do what she always did when she felt nervous: she took a deep breath, straightened her shoulders, then carried on as if she had all the confidence in the world. She strode into the auditorium and tramped onto

The neon lights of Broadway attracted many aspiring actors and actresses who, like Barbra, searched for stardom in New York City's theater district.

the stage in her smudged tennis shoes and thrift-shop fur coat.

"My name is Barbra—with two *a*'s," she said loudly, squinting into the darkness. When a voice asked her to sing something, she reached for her pile of sheet music, which she promptly scattered all over the floor of the stage. This was not a promising start for a hopeful novice. As she scurried to gather up her music, she thought she heard laughter coming from the seemingly empty darkness before her. It hid the men slated to produce and direct a new musical comedy, *I Can Get It for You Wholesale*, based on the best-seller by Jerome Weidman about the New York garment district.

But Barbra was *undaunted*. She *knew* she had talent. Whenever she sang, people always stopped to listen, and they always asked to hear more. If there was one thing she was sure of, it was that she had a remarkable voice. With a quick flutter of her hand, she signaled the accompanist to begin. Then she fixed her eyes on a distant point in the darkness, took a deep breath, and sang "Value," a song from *Another Evening with Harry Stoones*. Her singing was unlike anything that anyone within earshot of the stage had ever heard before, with its shimmering, romantic intensity and its powerful, thrilling range. When the audition was finished and she sensed that it had been a success, Barbra excitedly pleaded from the stage, "Will somebody call me, please! Even if I don't get the part, just call!"

One of the invisible men seated beyond the footlights was Elliott Gould, the handsome young actor who had already been cast as the play's male lead. He was so impressed with Barbra's audition that later the same night, he telephoned her, identified himself, and said simply, "You were brilliant." Then he hung up.

Because she was a newcomer, Barbra was asked to four more auditions, but she eventually won the comedic role of Miss Marmelstein, the harassed yet loyal secretary in *I Can Get It for You Wholesale*. Yetta Tessye Marmelstein was supposed to be a frumpy 50-year-old spinster who, except for her single song, had only a minor role in the show. But director Arthur Laurents was determined not to waste a new singing and comedic talent as rare as Barbra's, so he immediately began rewriting the role to make the character more youthful and to give Barbra more time on stage.

As thrilled as Barbra was to have finally landed her first role in a Broadway musical—and as confident as she was in her singing talent—she also had some insecurities. She knew she was not a conventionally pretty woman. In fact, she had always considered herself homely because of her large, bumpy nose. As the play went into rehearsal, she found herself wishing that she could play a more attractive character, like the female ingenue portrayed by Sheree North. Director Laurents tried to reassure her, for he was certain that she was more talented than the rest of the cast. Privately, he expected her to steal the show on opening night.

In rehearsal with Elliott Gould and Jack Krushen for I Can Get It for You Wholesale. *Barbra's big break came when she landed a role in the Broadway show at the age of 19.*

During the rehearsals for *Wholesale*, Barbra continued to struggle with recurring feelings of insecurity about her appearance. Even the romantic attention of leading man Elliott Gould, although it excited and flattered her, did not make her feel attractive. She began to wonder if she had been given the role of Miss Marmelstein because she was *not* pretty. Since her childhood, Barbra had felt awkward and ugly, especially after she had confided to her mother that she wanted to be an actress, and her mother had flatly told her that she was not pretty enough to become famous. "In a sense," Barbra told *Playboy* magazine in 1977, "she's probably responsible for my success. Because I was always trying to prove to her that I was worthwhile, that I wasn't just a skinny little *marink*." Her uneasiness about her role in *Wholesale*, however, was not entirely unfounded. The producer, David Merrick, actually did find Barbra unattractive and privately referred to her as a "crazy-looking, ugly thing." He even thought of firing her, but he was vehemently overruled by director Laurents, composer Harold Rome, and author Jerome Weidman, who all insisted that she had remarkable singing talent.

The truth was that Barbra had felt like an outsider all her life. Her father had died when she was only 15 months old, and when her mother remarried, it was to a remote, unsympathetic man who took an immediate dislike to Barbra—as she did to him. From the depths of her unhappiness, she began plotting her revenge in the form of an escape from Flatbush (a district in the borough of Brooklyn) to Manhattan. Her nose may have been too large, her eyes slightly crossed, and her legs too skinny, but she could at least console herself with dreams of stardom.

Now, as she prepared for what she hoped would be the fulfillment of that dream, she veered between episodes of serious and foolish behavior. On some days she arrived promptly for rehearsal, but on other days she was late and would playfully clown around, inventing lines for herself that were not in the musical's script. Perhaps her erratic antics were caused by simple immaturity: she was, after all, an inexperienced teenager who was suddenly surrounded by seasoned professionals. Or perhaps such behavior was a defense against her lifelong insecurity about her appearance. Whatever the reason, director Laurents finally became impatient and reprimanded her in front of the entire cast, demanding that she stick to her original lines and act more like a disciplined professional.

If Barbra felt the sting of his reprimand, she was too proud to let herself show it. She had a strong will and knew what felt right for her as a performer. Although she agreed to return to her scripted lines so as not to distract and disorient other members of the cast, she refused to sing her musical number standing up, as Laurents directed. Instead, she insisted on singing seated in a swivel chair—where, as she logically pointed out, Miss Marmelstein was likely to spend most of her day. When the company went on tour with *I Can Get It for You Wholesale*, Barbra and Laurents were still arguing about whether she should do her song standing up or sitting down. Finally, on the night of the play's tryout in Philadelphia, Barbra wore down his resistance. The director allowed her to do the song her way. That night her "Miss Marmelstein" number was a huge success, forever ending the dispute over whether she should sit or stand. For the skinny girl from Flatbush, it was an important victory.

Barbra's strong need to follow her own instincts and ambitions had taken her this far, enabling her to persevere against odds that would have discouraged most other young women. Outspoken and offbeat, she had pounded the pavements of New York City, going from one stage audition to another—only to be turned away most of the time because she lacked experience. Unable to afford her own apartment, she carried a folding cot around the city and slept at friends' apartments. To earn money for acting lessons at night, she spent her days working odd jobs like baby-sitting, ushering, and typing. When she lacked money for regular meals, she subsisted on yogurt. When she could not afford to buy department-store clothing, she bought second-hand clothes from thrift shops or borrowed friends' clothes.

Barbra was a fighter, driven by a need for the love she had never felt as a child, and for the recognition that her singing talent deserved. She knew that she wanted to become a living legend in her own time. Nothing—not an odd physical appearance, a Brooklyn accent, or an empty pocketbook—would make her compromise her obsessive pursuit of stardom. She was a demanding per-

From her secretarial chair, Barbra sings Miss Marmelstein's three-minute lament in I Can Get It for You Wholesale. *Her performance stopped the show and made Streisand an overnight sensation.*

fectionist who was willing to battle her way to the top.

On March 22, 1962, four months after Barbra's audition, *I Can Get It for You Wholesale* opened at the Shubert Theatre on Broadway. Set in the ruthless world of New York's Seventh Avenue garment district, the show was not destined to run very long. One number in the second act, however, stopped the show on opening night and at every subsequent performance during the production's nine-month run. That number was the song of the oppressed secretary, Miss Marmelstein. On opening night, after Barbra had finished her song, there was complete silence. Then came the deafening whipcrack of wild applause as the audience rose to its feet and cried, "Bravo!" A friend of Streisand who was present at that night's performance would later recall, "I saw her on opening night in *Wholesale*, and she literally stopped the show. People were on their feet screaming and yelling for five minutes. It was eerie. It was electrifying."

The critics who saw the show gave it mixed reviews, yet on one point they all agreed: the 19-year-old new-comer with the Brooklyn accent and the big voice had given an unforgettable performance. Norman Nadel of the *New York World Telegram* suggested that Barbra's alma mater, Brooklyn's Erasmus Hall High School, "should call a half-day holiday to celebrate the success of its spectacular alumna, 19-year-old Barbra Streisand." Howard Taubman, theater critic for the *New York Times*, wrote, "The evening's find is Barbra Streisand."

People in the audience were not sure exactly who Barbra Streisand was, but they probably sensed that she was destined to become a star. With just three minutes to present Yetta Marmelstein's comic lament in song, Barbra managed to completely engage the audience's sympathy. Throughout the show's run, Barbra's musical number was the only one that brought down the house at every performance. According to Arthur Laurents, whenever she would come on the stage, "there were fireworks."

After her spectacularly successful debut in *Wholesale*, articles about Barbra appeared in national magazines such as *Time* and *Life*, and she became a popular guest on a variety of television talk shows. She was the only member of the *Wholesale* cast nominated for a Tony award. Although she did not win the Tony, she did receive the New York Drama Critics' Circle Award for Best Supporting Actress.

Now that her career in show business was taking off, Barbra responded with a mixture of disbelief and euphoria. When the breaks she had been waiting for finally came, she felt a surge of determination that was stronger than ever. "They tell me I'll eventually win everything, the Emmy for TV, the Grammy for records, the Tony for Broadway and the Oscar for movies," she giddily enthused. "It would be wonderful to win all those awards, to be rich and to have my name on marquees all over the world."

All of those things would actually come to pass in the years that followed. But at that time, the legend was just wishful thinking. With intelligence, independence, and a defiant will to succeed, Barbra devoted herself to the process of achieving stardom. Not only did she become a successful singer whose album sales set new records in the music industry but she also evolved into an accomplished actress who handled both comic and dramatic roles with ease. Moreover, she emerged as one of the first women in the United States to establish herself in the traditionally male-dominated fields of movie directing and producing.

For more than 30 years, Barbra Streisand has endured as one of America's most talented and successful stars. She is now the living legend she once dreamed of becoming when she was just another girl from Brooklyn.

Flatbush, Brooklyn, as it appeared when Barbara Joan Streisand was a young girl.

2

THE GIRL
FROM BROOKLYN

It would be hard to imagine a more secure or welcoming environment than the one into which Barbara (as her name was spelled) Joan Streisand was born on April 24, 1942. Her parents, Emmanuel and Diana, were a vigorous, handsome couple and they were deeply in love. Emmanuel Streisand, the son of a fish dealer, taught English at the George Westinghouse Vocational High School in Brooklyn, where he was popular with both students and colleagues alike. Determined to make an even better life for his family, he was also studying for a graduate degree in education from Columbia University. His wife, Diana Rosen Streisand, was the daughter of a tailor who was also a cantor at the local synagogue. Diana had a beautiful voice and had considered becoming a professional singer. Once she met and married "Manny," then an athletic, darkly handsome student, she put aside dreams of a singing career and happily devoted herself to being a wife and mother.

Although they had little money when they married in 1930, Diana and Emmanuel were hopeful about their future and planned their life together with care. Concerned about their economic stability, they timed the arrival of both of their children, waiting five years after their marriage to have Sheldon, and seven years after his birth to have Barbara. When their beautiful new daughter arrived, their happiness seemed complete.

But that happiness was cruelly shattered in the summer of 1943. Hoping to earn some extra money while giving his young family a vacation in the country, Barbara's father accepted a job as head counselor at a camp in upstate New York. Although Diana Streisand was no lover of the outdoors, preferring the cozy security of their apartment, she packed up the children and accompanied her husband to the Catskill Mountains. At the camp, Barbara's father threw himself into his job with gusto. He employed both his teaching and athletic skills with energy and confidence, even taking over the duties of several counselors who unexpectedly quit. Although his health appeared to be excellent, Manny Streisand suddenly collapsed and died on August 3— the official cause of death was respiratory failure, which occurred because of improper treatment of an epileptic seizure. Manny's abrupt death at the age of 34 left Diana and her two young children with a hole at the center of their lives.

Although Diana was devastated by the loss of her beloved husband, she struggled to put the pieces of her life back together. The most pressing problem she faced was that of economic survival. Since she could no longer afford the family's comfortable apartment on Schenectady Avenue, she and the children moved in with her parents on Pulaski Street in the Bedford-Stuyvesant area of Brooklyn. At first she was able to support her children on her brother's army allotment checks, but when World War II ended and his checks stopped, she found work as a bookkeeper.

Now Barbara and her brother, Sheldon, were left all day with their grandparents, who were stern caretakers. "I remember there was a huge table in the dining

room and Barbara and I would scuttle under it to avoid beatings," Sheldon later recalled. His sister would remember how money was always in short supply. "We were poor, but not *poor* poor. We just never had anything." The relationship between Barbara and her mother also grew increasingly strained. Although the young girl desperately needed her mother's affection and approval, Diana Streisand had withdrawn into her grief over her husband's death. While she remained a dutiful mother to Barbara, she was not especially loving or demonstrative.

The distance between them widened further in 1950 when Barbara was eight years old and Diana married Louis Kind, a man Barbara first met during a stay at summer camp when her mother brought him along for

Streisand was the middle child of the family— between brother Sheldon, who was seven years older, and half sister Roslyn, who was eight years younger. Because young Barbara did not get along with her stepfather, Louis Kind, she often felt isolated from the family, although the siblings would be closer when they were older.

Jean Simmons and Marlon Brando in the 1955 Broadway musical–based film Guys and Dolls, *one of Barbara's favorite films as a teenager. At the movies she could escape an unhappy childhood, as she imagined herself in the role of each leading lady.*

a visit. Barbara disliked him from the moment she saw him. Since her father's death, she had dreaded the prospect of her mother's remarriage, and now that nightmare was coming true. Kind moved his new family out of Bedford-Stuyvesant into a six-story apartment building in Flatbush at the corner of Newkirk and Nostrand Avenues. He sensed right from the start that his stepdaughter hated him, and he responded by ignoring her as much as possible. Sometimes he was deliberately cruel. Once he refused to give her an ice cream cone, saying she was too ugly. After Diana gave birth to a daughter, Roslyn, he seemed to enjoy taunting Barbara by comparing her unfavorably to her new sister. Striving to please her new husband, Diana also favored Roslyn. Soon Barbara began to feel like an intruder in her own family.

But she was resourceful in finding ways to escape her unhappiness at home. Every Saturday afternoon she headed for the neighborhood Loew's Kings Theater on Flatbush Avenue. There, munching on a Mello-roll (a marshmallow and ice cream confection), she would gaze intently at the big screen and lose herself in the fantasy of being a beautiful, alluring woman who was adored by a handsome, romantic man. One of her favorite movies was *Guys and Dolls.* As she listened to her idol Marlon Brando singing, "I'll know when my love comes along," she closed her eyes and imagined he was singing not to the actress Jean Simmons, but to her. Barbara later recalled that as she watched these movies, she could actually feel herself becoming the heroine: "I was not Vivien Leigh, I was Scarlett O'Hara, and I loved being the most beautiful woman kissed by the beautiful man."

When the movies ended, stepping out of the glamorous, romantic world inside the darkened theater and back into the harsh daylight of the drab city streets was a bitter adjustment. "My mother hated it when I went to the movies," Streisand has said. "I was always grouchy for a couple of days afterward. After looking at all those beautiful clothes, apartments, and furniture, coming back to the place where we lived used to depress me."

Intent on prolonging the fantasies of opulent perfection that she had seen on-screen, Barbara would lock herself in the bathroom when she returned to her modest two-bedroom apartment. She would then stand in front of the mirror for hours impersonating Judy Garland or Marilyn Monroe, pretending she had the sophisticated good looks of an Elizabeth Taylor or an Audrey Hepburn. As she grew older, Barbara tried to remake her own image so that she more closely resembled the physical ideal of female Hollywood stardom. She experimented with sultry hair styles and applied heavy layers of mascara and eye shadow for a more exotic look. Someday, she vowed to herself, it would be *her* name blazing in lights up there on the marquee of the Loew's Kings Theater.

In 1954, as Barbara was about to enter adolescence, Louis Kind separated from Diana, leaving her and her three children alone. Barbara felt relief, but she also felt a resurgence of curiosity about her real father, Emmanuel Streisand. Years later, she would reflect, "When a kid grows up missing one parent, there's a big gap that has to be filled. . . . I felt more, I sensed more, I wanted more." Now Barbara's yearning for stardom became more purposeful. She would not just dream of being a glamorous actress; she would take the necessary steps to become one.

Barbara was not the only freshman entering Erasmus Hall High School in the fall of 1955 with lofty ambitions. Erasmus was a public school with an outstanding reputation: many of its graduates went on to become famous in the arts, including actress Barbara Stanwyck. As a freshman, Barbara created an immediate sensation. Not only was she an excellent student, but her unusual way of dressing and her offbeat behavior attracted considerable attention. Although Barbara joined the Choral Club, she scorned participation in the school's theatrical productions, thinking them too amateurish. She preferred professional auditions. At the age of 13 she tried out for a part in a radio program, performing a speech from *Saint Joan.*

In the spring of Barbara's freshman year, she saw her first Broadway play, *The Diary of Anne Frank.* As she sat in the audience watching Susan Strasberg portray the doomed Jewish schoolgirl, Barbara felt a shock of recognition. Like Anne, she too wanted to escape from a confining circumstance, fall in love, and grow up to do meaningful work. And like Anne, Barbara hoped to make a name for herself that would live on after her death.

Although the play ends tragically, Barbara's first contact with the Broadway stage thrilled her. She left the theater in a rosy haze of enchantment. With all of her mind and heart, she knew that she could perform for an audience as unforgettably as the actors and actresses she had just seen onstage. Sitting on the train back to Brooklyn that night, she was convinced more than ever before that the life of an actress was her destiny.

Barbara's first chance to appear in a professional play came in the summer of 1957 when, pretending to be 17 instead of her actual age of 15, she won a summer stock position with the Malden Bridge Playhouse in upstate New York. It was Barbara's first real taste of the acting life, and she loved every minute of it, whether she was assigned to be a janitor, stagehand, or actress. Cast as the flirtatious secretary in *Desk Set*, she exuberantly threw herself into the role. Her enthusiasm was rewarded with her first positive review, which read, "The girl who plays the office vamp is very sexy, and her name is Barbara Streisand. Down boys!" When the summer ended, it was no easy task for her to return to her dingy apartment in Brooklyn and sleep on the living room couch again.

STREISAND, BARBARA
Freshman Chorus, 1, 2; Choral Club, 2-4.

To join the New York theater world as soon as she could, Barbara completed high school six months early. Other famous graduates of Erasmus Hall High School in Brooklyn include chess wiz Bobby Fischer, actress Barbara Stanwyck, and singer Neil Diamond.

But Barbara found a new escape when she landed a job as a cashier at Choy's Chinese, a local restaurant run by her neighbors, Jimmy and Muriel Choy. She became especially close to Muriel, whose daughters she had baby-sat in the past. The job gave her a chance to indulge her passion for Chinese food, which she continued to crave many years later. She also enjoyed the challenge of feeling like a cultural outsider. "I loved the idea of belonging to a small minority group," she said. "It was the world against us in the Chinese restaurant."

By her junior year in high school, Barbara was often taking the train into Manhattan alone. There she found a whole new world waiting for her, one that included not only the theater but also classical music, art, and literature. She would later remember, "I became consumed with acting and used to go to the New York

Anne Frank, played by Susan Strasberg, receives a kiss from her father, played by Joseph Schildkraut, in the 1956 performance of The Diary of Anne Frank. *The Broadway drama inspired Barbara to dream of the day she too would perform on the stage.*

Public Library. . . . I read Russian plays, Russian novels, Greek tragedies. *Anna Karenina* changed my life." She developed a burning desire to move to Manhattan, where she felt she could lead the exciting life she dreamed of. Scanning the apartment ads in the newspaper, she would plead with her mother, "Ma, look, it's $105, why can't we afford it?"

But her mother was eager for her to get good grades and behave like a proper Jewish schoolgirl. Although Barbara was in honors classes and hung out with the smartest students, she considered herself a social misfit. "I had violet lips, blue eyes and then I bleached the top of my hair blonde," she recalls. "They used to call me Colorful, because I had all this color on me. I was pathetically skinny in these long dresses. I looked funny." She also had the longest fingernails of any girl in her high school, defiantly grown after her mother's suggestion that Barbara become a secretary instead of an actress. Sporting nails several inches long, she could not possibly learn how to type.

Meanwhile, Barbara's subway rides into Manhattan continued. Her next discovery was Greenwich Village, where she took a job as a volunteer stagehand at the Cherry Lane Theatre. There she befriended one of the actresses, Anita Miller, whose husband was a drama coach in the city. Impressed by Barbara's intensity and drive to succeed in the theater, Anita brought her home one night to audition for her husband. Although Barbara's performance was awkward and undisciplined, Allan Miller was so struck by the depth of her yearning to become an actress that he offered her free acting lessons. Barbara quickly accepted.

In exchange for being in Miller's Theater Studio Workshop, Barbara offered to baby-sit for Anita and Allan's two children. She began to stay with the

Millers, commuting to her high school classes in Brooklyn. In the summer of 1958, Barbara went with the Millers when they performed in summer stock at the Clinton Playhouse, in Clinton, Connecticut. Not only did Barbara continue to help care for the children, but she also appeared in the playhouse's production of *Tobacco Road*. The chance to be onstage again exhilarated her and made her yearn even more intensely for a theatrical career.

Now that she had begun to make a new life for herself in New York, Barbara was impatient to leave behind her high school days. By attending summer school and taking some extra credit courses, she was able to graduate a semester early—in January 1959—from Erasmus Hall High. Barbara's grade average was 93 and she was awarded a medal in Spanish. Next she announced to her mother that she was moving into Manhattan so she could find work in the theater. Diana Kind was still opposed to Barbara's striking out on her own at such a young age, but she finally relented. By this time she realized that she was destined to lose a battle of wills against her headstrong daughter. Privately, however, she feared that Barbara was taking a big risk trying to break into show business when she would be competing with so many girls who were prettier than she was.

After graduation Barbara decided that the time had come to leave the Miller family and find her own apartment. When she discovered that Susan Dworkowitz, a friend from high school, needed a roommate for an apartment on 34th Street, Barbara happily moved in with her. Although she still had very little money and would have to take a series of subsistence jobs to survive, she walked the city streets in a state of euphoria. At last she was creating a life that would make all her dreams come true.

A romance bloomed between Elliott Gould and Barbra Streisand when they met during the 1962 production of the Broadway musical I Can Get It for You Wholesale.

3

LOVE AND FAME

Once she had settled into her apartment, Barbara established the routine she would follow for the next few years. By day she supported herself with a series of tedious clerical and secretarial jobs; then at night she would grab a carton of yogurt or a hamburger and race off to acting lessons. For a while she continued to study with Allan Miller, but she eventually began studying with another acting coach, Eli Rill. Both drama instructors had been members of the New York Actors Studio, headed by Lee Strasberg, considered a master of theater technique. At 15 Barbara had auditioned for the Actors Studio but had been turned down.

When her roommate returned to Brooklyn, Barbara was forced to move again, this time into a walk-up apartment on West 48th Street. With the encouragement of drama coaches Miller and Rill, she began to make the rounds of theatrical auditions in earnest. She would check magazines like *Show Business* for upcoming casting calls, then show up at them wearing the outlandish clothing that she considered her trademark. But as an unknown, she was usually dismissed and not even given a chance to read. In desperation she finally resorted to trying out for walk-on parts, which had no lines

The Actors Studio was headed by renowned actor Lee Strasberg, who taught many famous performers, including Marlon Brando and Marilyn Monroe. Young Streisand had difficulty gaining recognition as an actress: she applied for the Studio but was not accepted, although she did study with two of its members, Allan Miller and Eli Rill.

or dialogue, but her efforts were still unsuccessful.

Streisand needed a new strategy if she was going to break through the iron barrier of New York's theatrical world. So she began to think of singing as a possible way of achieving recognition. "I hated singing—I wanted to be an actress," she later recalled. "But I don't think I would have made it any other way."

In the summer of 1960, Barbara entered a talent contest at The Lion, a gay bar and restaurant on West Ninth Street in Greenwich Village. First prize was $50 a week for a two-week singing engagement, with free meals included. If she won, she could not only be seen by casting people there but also make some money. When Barbara signed up for the talent contest, she changed the spelling of her name, dropping the second *a* to become Barbra. She then rehearsed in front of friends, and prepared her own renditions of the ballad "A Sleepin' Bee" and a song that one of her idols, Johnny Mathis, had made famous, "When Sunny Gets Blue."

On the hot June morning of The Lion talent show audition, it was a newly named Barbra Streisand who stepped up to the microphone. She had never before sung for a public audience or even had a formal singing lesson in her life. But after she had sung only a few lines of her first song, the incredulous manager of The Lion knew that the contest was over. "We just couldn't believe what we were hearing," he remembers. "When she finished, I said to her . . .'That was really magnificent!'" She easily won the competition.

Later that night, Barbra created a sensation with her first performance in front of an audience at the bar. So great was her success at The Lion that her engagement there was extended. Word quickly spread among the bar's regular clientele that a new singing sensation was performing, and people began packing the tiny room where Barbra sang every night. One evening Allan and Anita Miller came. When Barbra started to sing, they could hardly believe their ears. They knew her only as an actress; they had never suspected she could sing.

Shortly after her engagement at The Lion ended, Barbra was signed up by the Bon Soir, a larger nightclub where the Village "smart set" gathered. Barbra kept the song "A Sleepin' Bee" in her act, but she also added some new ones, such as "Cry Me a River" and her own madcap version of "Who's Afraid of the Big, Bad Wolf?" Although she had altered her first name, she refused to change her last name because when she became a star, she wanted everyone who had known her back in Brooklyn to recognize her name.

Barbra's appearance at the Bon Soir began on Labor Day weekend, 1960, and was so remarkably successful that it was extended from two to eleven weeks. People eagerly crowded into the cellar club every night to hear the rich, emotive voice that was so unlike any other they had heard. The essence of Barbra's magic was her theatrical style of presenting each song. She approached every new set of lyrics as if they were being spoken by a character in a play that she had to interpret for an audience. "I always wanted to be an actress, that's why lyrics are so important to me," Barbra has said. "I am drawn to songs that have a place to go, songs that have a beginning, middle and end. They are like mini-theatrical pieces."

Barbra would pretend to herself that she was creating a specific dramatic role when she sang a song. For example, she tried to imagine the face of one particular person, to whom she would address an impassioned lament like "Cry Me a River." The effect on her audiences was electrifying. "I'm an actress who sings," Barbra has often said of herself. Whenever she sang, she knew it was in her power to make an audience laugh or cry just as if she were an actress performing a dramatic piece.

At the Bon Soir, Barbra attracted the attention of several talent agents. One was Ted Rozar. In the spring of 1961, with the help of another agent, Irvin Arthur, he arranged for Barbra to go on a tour that included relatively small bookings in places like Detroit, San Francisco, and St. Louis. But Barbra became dissatisfied with Rozar's efforts. So she turned for help to another agent who had approached her at the Bon Soir—Marty Erlichman. He had a warm, fatherly personality that put her at ease, and he was also able to negotiate more lucrative bookings for her. Their association was a successful one that would last for decades.

Barbra soon began appearing on several television shows. On April 5, 1961, she made her debut on her first national television program, *The Jack Paar Show*. In the following months she became a regular on several other New York–based television talk-show programs including Mike Wallace's *P.M. East* and *The*

Barbra's success at The Lion talent show led to other nightclub performances, such as one pictured here at the Bon Soir.

David Susskind Show. In May she returned to the Bon
Soir, opening with the comedienne Renee Taylor. This
time Barbra's performance was reviewed by *New York
Times* critic Arthur Gelb, who called her "a wonderful
new singer."

But Barbra was still dreaming of Broadway. When the
creators of a new off-Broadway revue, *Another Evening
with Harry Stoones*, began casting, Marty Erlichman
arranged for Barbra to audition. The show's writer, Jeff
Harris, and its musical director, Abba Bogin, were looking for talented, versatile performers who could sing,
dance, and be funny. "Let's grab her. She's fantastic,"
said Harris when Barbra's tryout ended. Her comic
instinct and her full, rich voice were just what they were
looking for, and she was promptly hired.

On Saturday, October 21, 1961, the revue opened at
the Gramercy Arts Theatre with spirited performances
from the entire cast and a showstopping solo, "Value,"
sung by Streisand. But the critics were not impressed.
The next morning after both the *New York Times* and
the *Herald Tribune* had panned the show, the producers decided to close it after just one performance.

Despite the early closing of the show, Streisand had
been noticed, and several later reviews of *Harry Stoones*
singled her out for high praise. A scant month later,
Barbra was back in the spotlight, opening at the Blue
Angel, a chic midtown supper club where some of the
most important producers in show business came to
look for new talent. One night Arthur Laurents, the
director of a new Broadway musical, *I Can Get It for
You Wholesale*, happened to be in the audience at the
Blue Angel during Barbra's performance. Her offbeat
manner and big, thrilling voice made him think of her
right away as a possibility for the role of the secretary,
Miss Marmelstein, in the new musical he was casting.
He promptly arranged for an audition.

That solicited Broadway audition eventually won
Barbra the part of Yetta Tessye Marmelstein. Jerome

Weidman, who adopted his novel for the stage, recalls the sensational impact of Barbra's first audition for *Wholesale*: "When we heard this kid, she just knocked us off our ears. Harold Rome and I sat down and immediately expanded the role. You see when you have a talent that large on stage, you just can't let her wander around."

By the time *I Can Get It for You Wholesale* went into rehearsal, Barbra and Elliott Gould were beginning to spend more time together. He would walk her to the subway every day, although he was initially too shy to ask her for a date. "She scared me," he remembered, "But I really dug her. I think I was the first person who ever did." He continued, "What is appealing about Barbra is that underneath that façade is the most sensitive child-girl I have ever met." Gradually they discovered that their interests were a good match. Both loved Chinese restaurants, horror movies, and poking about in thrift shops or penny arcades. Sometimes they would just take long walks together in the snow or go watch the skaters at Rockefeller Center. One night after Elliott and Barbra had a playful snowball fight, he gently put snow on her face and kissed her. "She was the most innocent thing I'd ever seen, like a beautiful flower that hadn't blossomed yet," he said later.

But their romance hit a roadblock when Barbra imagined that Elliott was flirting with another girl in the show. One day after rehearsal, she stopped speaking to him. Later that night, whenever he tried to call her, she hung up. Finally, he gave up and went to bed, but at 4:00 A.M. his doorbell rang. When he answered it, there stood a bedraggled Barbra, crying and still wearing her nightgown.

That night Elliott walked her home to the tiny East Side apartment where she lived above a fish restaurant. Although he thought the location an odd place, within a few weeks, as their relationship grew more serious, he moved in with her. "The only window looked out on a

black brick wall," Gould recalled. "We used to eat on the sewing machine. A big rat named Oscar lived in the kitchen." The rooms were filled with Barbra's strange thrift-shop purchases—a broken-down dentist's cabinet, empty picture frames, and a scattered assortment of antique satin lingerie, feather boas, and fur coats.

On March 22, 1962, the opening night of *I Can Get It for You Wholesale*, it came as no surprise to anyone in the cast when Barbra stole the show. Most people attributed its subsequent nine-month run to the strength of her performance alone. But she worried privately about the effect that her triumph would have on her romance with Elliott, who was struggling to launch his own show business career. "I had very mixed feelings," she says of her success in *Wholesale*. "On the one hand, I loved it; on the other hand, I hated it because I didn't want Elliott to be hurt."

Although she had just a minor part in I Can Get It for You Wholesale, *newcomer Streisand won the New York Drama Critics' Circle Award and received a Tony nomination for her performance.*

The Ed Sullivan Show, *television's longest running variety show, aired on Sunday nights for 23 years. Perhaps best known for introducing the English group The Beatles to America, the variety show showcased many other stars, including a young singer named Barbra Streisand.*

The recognition she received for her performance was not limited to nightly standing ovations in the Shubert Theatre. Two weeks after the show opened, she received a Tony nomination for Best Supporting Actress in a Musical. Although Phyllis Newman won the award for her performance in *Subways Are for Sleeping,* Barbra did go on to receive the New York Drama Critics' Circle Award. She also continued to perform on New York–based television programs, such as *The Joe Franklin Show.* As the months passed and she began to grow bored with the role of an unattractive secretary, she turned once more to club appearances, singing at the Bon Soir in May 1962, and as the headline attraction at the Blue Angel for the summer. Adding numbers like "Much More" from *The Fantastiks* and Leonard Bernstein's "Songs for Children," she expanded her repertoire to include more serious than comic songs. She savored the chance to feel glamorous onstage, and to perform pieces that she chose, rather than being restricted by the rigid confines of the same role and the same song night after night.

When *Wholesale* finally closed in December 1962, Barbra was determined to use her Broadway success to invigorate her show business career. On January 23, 1963, she began a three-day session in the recording studio of Columbia Records to make her debut record, *The Barbra Streisand Album.* When it was released a month later, she embarked on a promotional tour to boost its success, starting at the Blue Angel in New York and moving to the Hungry i in San Francisco.

Unlike her first tour two years earlier, this one was an overwhelming success. Her fee had now jumped to $7,500 per week, and critics responded to the vibrant versatility of her act with rave reviews. After her appearance at the Hungry i, critic Owen Huddleson wrote,

"Once in a lifetime, if you are lucky, you are able to witness the birth of a new star in the entertainment world. . . . Miss Streisand is a solid personality who has the talent to become one of the all-time singing greats in show business."

The Barbra Streisand Album was such a success that Columbia agreed to release her second album by the end of the year. Meanwhile, Barbra's public triumphs continued to multiply. Summer began with her smash appearance on *The Ed Sullivan Show* on June 9, 1963. Then on August 21, she opened at the Cocoanut Grove in the Ambassador Hotel in Los Angeles. Although she disliked having to perform in a noisy dinner club atmosphere, she knew this was probably her most important club appearance yet. Wearing a smartly stylish gingham gown that she had designed just for her act there, she sang the mesmerizing ballad, "When the Sun Comes Out." Not only did everyone stop eating when she began to sing, but the waiters were so entranced by her beautiful voice that they stopped serving. She completed her tour with a sold-out performance at the Arie Crown Theatre in Chicago.

Now that her concert tour success was established and her album was breaking records on the sales charts, she and Elliott felt the time had come to marry. Once their decision was made, they acted quickly. Elliott had just returned from London, where he had starred in a production of *Our Town*: the separation had made them realize how much they wanted to be together. "It was like we shook on it. Let's get married—glop! So we did," remembered Gould. On September 13, 1963, they married in Carson City, Nevada (Barbra was completing an engagement at Harrah's in nearby Lake Tahoe).

Barbra's contentment now seemed complete. She had the star status and the handsome, attentive husband she had always dreamed of. But actually her dreams had only just begun to come true.

When she signed to do the Broadway show Funny Girl, *Barbra Streisand went from supporting player to star. Her reputation was so firmly established that the show's cast album reached number two on the* Billboard *chart—before the musical even opened.*

4

FUNNY GIRL

Barbra Streisand had now triumphed on Broadway and in sold-out singing engagements at major nightclubs all over the country, but she wanted to demonstrate her appeal to television audiences. Her regular guest appearances on New York late-night television shows such as Mike Wallace's *P.M. East* and *The David Susskind Show* had fostered Barbra's image as an eccentric, nonconforming young woman who bluntly spoke her mind but who could also belt out romantic songs in an enthralling style. She gradually made the transition from local shows to national TV, appearing on weekly programs hosted by Dinah Shore, Ed Sullivan, Garry Moore, and Bob Hope. On October 6, 1963, she appeared on the new *Judy Garland Show* in a performance that would make television history.

When the legendary singer Judy Garland had first heard reports that her potential successor, "the new Garland," was performing at the Cocoanut Grove, she had gone to Barbra's closing night performance with some apprehension. What she saw did stir feelings of rivalry, yet she was also moved by the Streisand sound.

Garland began to wonder how her version of the song "Get

Happy" would sound if it were combined with Streisand's melancholy interpretation of "Happy Days Are Here Again." She found out a few months later, when she stood on the stage next to Barbra as the two sang a soulful, memorable duet. The song was the thrilling high point of an hour that left Garland's audience spellbound. Barbra's performance was so good that she won an Emmy nomination for Outstanding Performance in a Variety or Musical Program. It was the first time a performer making a guest appearance had earned such a nomination.

Barbra next returned to Broadway to prepare for her new role in a musical based on the life of the legendary Ziegfield Follies star Fanny Brice. Ray Stark, Brice's son-in-law, was a well-known movie producer who had wanted to bring the life story of his famous mother-in-law to the Broadway stage for some time. When he finally found a version of Fanny Brice's story that he liked, in the form of a play written by Isobel Lennart, he decided to make his Broadway production debut. Stark collaborated with musical writer Jule Styne and directors Garson Kanin and Jerome Robbins. Although Stark had originally imagined Anne Bancroft or Carol Burnett in the role, after seven long auditions, he finally cast Streisand—who actually did bear a striking physical resemblance to Fanny Brice—as the musical's lead.

Now that she had won the role that would seal her stage career, Streisand needed a home worthy of a Broadway diva. Her drab railroad flat above the fish restaurant was not a suitable address for a rising star. She was too busy with concert engagements to look for a new home, however, so Elliott volunteered to house-hunt for her. The minute she saw his first choice, an elegant duplex at 320 Central Park West, she was enchanted. Not only did the penthouse have the dramatic winding staircase she had always dreamed of, but its huge balcony, situated 21 stories above the ground, offered a breathtaking view of Manhattan.

After moving into the luxurious duplex, she and Elliott busily began filling it with furniture. Now that Barbra could afford it, she shopped in antique stores rather than thrift shops. Her most prized find was an ornately carved 300-year-old bed that she had mounted on a dais and draped in damask. Adding her own personal touch to the piece, Barbra had a small refrigerator built into it where she stored her beloved coffee ice cream.

As *Funny Girl* entered rehearsals in December, Streisand looked back on 1963 with both satisfaction and disbelief. She had been named Best Female Vocalist of 1963 and also *Cue* magazine's Entertainer of the Year. The stunning power, clarity, and sweetness of her voice, as well as her ability to dramatize lyrics, had made remarkable successes of her first two albums—*The Barbra Streisand Album,* released in March, and *The Second Barbra Streisand Album,* released in August—even though she had not yet recorded a hit single. *Cash Box* magazine wrote, "The Streisand name could be the biggest to hit show business since Elvis Presley." She was on her way to becoming a sensation, both on Broadway and in the recording industry.

At the end of December, as the *Funny Girl* cast prepared to leave rehearsals at the Winter Garden Theatre and head for tryouts in Boston, rumors had begun to fly that the show was in trouble. For one thing, it was too long and needed to be cut. But the show's length was not the only problem: there was talk that Streisand was struggling with the role of Fanny Brice. Garson Kanin's

In fall of 1963, Barbra Streisand appeared on The Judy Garland Show, *where she and her host sang a medley combining "Happy Days Are Here Again" and "Get Happy." "Happy Days" would become one of Barbra's signature songs.*

Barbra Streisand rehearses with Funny Girl *lyricist Bob Merrill (right) and composer Jule Styne (at the piano).*

style was not to overdirect her. The result was that Barbra, who was still a relatively inexperienced actress, had difficulty in the scenes that required her simply to act and not sing. But when her former acting coach, Allan Miller, was called in to help her, she began to gain confidence in interpreting the role. She had always been a quick study with strong performing instincts.

Gradually the kinks in the production were resolved during its out-of-town run. Isobel Lennart rewrote the scenes that needed adjustment, and Jerome Robbins made cuts that helped the show's musical numbers move more quickly. Barbra worked incredibly hard during this period and actually seemed to relish the continual flux of the rewrites and last-minute changes. She recalls, "The more they changed the scenes, the more I liked it. The more I had different songs to try out, the more I loved it. We had 41 different last scenes, the last one being frozen only on opening night. Forty-one versions of a last scene! That was always exciting, stimulating." The result of all these changes was that Barbra's role became the very heart of the show, with her character appearing in virtually every scene. By the time the show was ready to open on Broadway, she felt the almost overwhelming pressure of knowing that the success or failure of the show depended on her performance.

After four postponements, *Funny Girl* finally opened at the Winter Garden Theatre on March 26, 1964. From the moment Barbra first appeared onstage, the delighted audience knew that the star and her role were a perfect fit. Barbra's portrayal of Fanny Brice was an extraordinary debut that inspired nothing but rave reviews. "Some stars merely brightened up a marquee: Barbra Streisand sets an entire theater ablaze," wrote a critic in *Time*. Whitney Bolton of the *Morning Telegraph* said, "Barbra Streisand . . . is talent, total, complete, utter and practicing. Vast talent, the kind that comes once in many years."

Overnight, Barbra had become a major celebrity. Every day she was mobbed by fans when she arrived at the theater and again after each performance as she tried to leave. The tale of the poor girl from Brooklyn who had suddenly become a star captured the imagination of an American public eager for a new Cinderella success story.

There was even an exotic "Streisand look" that some women tried to imitate: long, painted fingernails; bouffant-styled hair; and eyes made up to look like Cleopatra. To Barbra's amazement, her campy thrift-shop outfits were now considered fashionable, and her distinctive look was featured in cover stories of magazines like *Vogue, Life, Look, Time,* and *Newsweek.* Barbra's style was seen as ultramodern, and the *Encyclopedia Britannica* named her as one of two fashion trendsetters of the year.

On the night of May 12, 1964, Barbra achieved another major milestone in her musical career when she won two Grammy awards, one for the best vocal performance by a woman, and another for Best Album of the Year for her first release, *The Barbra Streisand Album.* Such important recognition from the recording industry helped to make up for losing an Emmy to Danny Kaye on May 25 and a Tony the night before to Carol Channing for *Hello, Dolly!*

Barbra's earning power had risen dramatically with her success. Only two years earlier, she had been paid $200 per week for her performance as Miss Marmelstein in *I Can Get It for You Wholesale.* As Fanny Brice in *Funny Girl,* she earned $5 thousand a week. Requests for concert engagements poured into the office of her manager, Marty Erlichman, some offering as much as $50 thousand a night. In the summer of 1964, the CBS television network announced that Streisand would be paid $5 million for doing 10 specials over a 10-year period.

Barbra's lifestyle clearly reflected her new prosperity. She now had a personal staff that included a full-time cook and a personal secretary. During the day, interior decorators often dropped by to leave upholstery or wallpaper samples as she indulged her passion for home decorating. Her life was changing with such speed that at times Barbra seemed bewildered by her own good fortune. In an interview with Shana Alexander during this period, she commented, "There's been no inter-mediate stages in my life. . . . I went direct from a rail-road flat to a duplex apartment."

By the end of 1964, she had proven her popularity as a recording artist. *Barbra Streisand/The Third Album,* a soft, melancholy release, eventually went to number five on the *Billboard* chart. The *Funny Girl* album, released shortly after the show's opening in March, was an even more spectacular hit, occupying the number two position in the *Billboard* chart and remaining there for five weeks. It would go on to win her a second Grammy for Best Female Pop Vocalist. During one week in October, no fewer than five Streisand record-ings were listed in the Top 100 of *Cashbox* magazine. Barbra was so proud of this achievement that she hung a copy of that week's chart on a wall in her New York penthouse.

During the year that followed, Barbra's triumphs seemed only to increase. On April 26, 1965, her first television special, "My Name Is Barbra," aired on CBS. Barbra offered no famous guest stars to guarantee success in the ratings, preferring to make it a one-woman show. Clad alternately in high-fashion gowns, opulent furs, and funky thrift-shop boas, she clowned, quipped, and sang her heart out for an hour, performing her smash hit "People" and ending with her signature rendition of "Happy Days Are Here Again." Her daring gamble on herself paid off. "My Name Is Barbra" was a huge ratings success and drew yet another round of enraptured reviews. In a single night Barbra had extended her audience to 50 million viewers, who quickly became smitten with her stylish image and her remarkable versatility as a performer. Barbra herself found television fulfilling in a way that

With her first television special, "My Name Is Barbra," Streisand received her first and second Emmy Awards in 1965.

Broadway and concert appearances were not. "So many times on the stage you reach a moment of truth in a scene and then it's gone," she said. "You know it's right, but you can't be sure of ever capturing it again. It's a very satisfying feeling to know that your work, your very hardest efforts, are preserved."

"My Name Is Barbra" won five Emmy Awards, including ones for concept, choreography, and staging, which especially pleased Barbra because she had negotiated hard for the right of complete creative control, trying to create a show that was a direct expression of her performing personality. Once again she had made television history. "My Name Is Barbra" changed forever the concept of the television special from a formula production that called for plenty of big-name guests into an innovative, versatile one-woman spectacular. Columbia Records released not one, but two albums of the special, the first of which earned Barbra her third personal Grammy.

For almost two years Barbra continued to play the role of Fanny Brice on Broadway. But the truth was, after the excitement of the opening weeks subsided, she had begun to grow bored with the show, just as she had during the run of *I Can Get It for You Wholesale.* "I had a big calendar; I would cross off the days," Barbra recalled. "After 18 months, all I wanted was out, out, out." Yet when she finally left the Broadway show in December 1965, it was to prepare for the same role in the London production of *Funny Girl,* which would open a few months later. Still, she welcomed the challenge of winning over London audiences and critics, both known for their exacting standards.

True to form, on the night of April 13, at the Prince of Wales Theatre, Barbra took London by storm. The British critics, who had initially been skeptical about the growing Streisand legend, became believers overnight. One said, "Barbra Streisand is a star, and *Funny Girl,* which had its official opening after the biggest buildup since D-Day, is her show." Another critic wondered what actress/singer could possibly play Barbra Streisand someday when the time came for a musical on her life. Barbra enjoyed the publicity, as well as the compliments of famous people such as Princess Margaret and actress Sophia Loren, both of whom came backstage to see her after her performance.

But once again, Barbra began to grow restless. Although she loved to perform onstage, she found the repetition of eight shows a week stifling. During this time, she mused aloud to *Funny Girl* costar Michael Craig, "Two and a half years ago when I started the show in Philadelphia it was such fun and everything was marvelous. Now it's all difficult and I don't get any fun out of it anymore."

Shortly after the show opened in London, Barbra discovered that she was pregnant. She and Elliott were

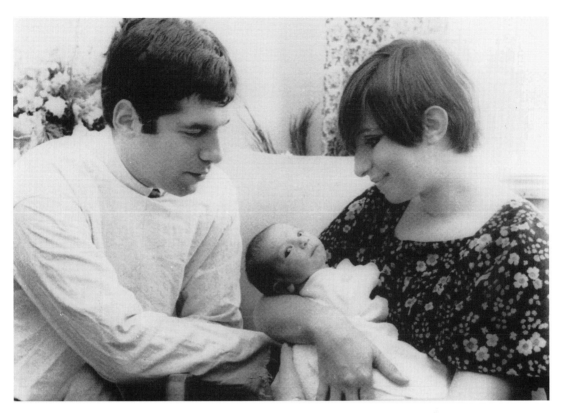

ecstatic. They both looked forward to the eventual change in their schedules that would permit them to settle into marriage and momentarily put aside the distractions of Barbra's stardom. On July 16, 1966, she gave her last performance in the London production of *Funny Girl* and immediately returned to New York to await the birth of her child. She cut back drastically on her singing schedule, although she did promote her new album, *Color Me Barbra*, and also performed some concerts in Atlanta, Philadelphia, and Chicago. In September, she also began recording a French-language album, *Je M'Appelle Barbra*.

On December 29, 1966, Jason Emmanuel Gould was born at Mt. Sinai Hospital in Manhattan. Although Barbra had prepared for natural childbirth, she had a difficult cesarean delivery. But when her seven-pound,

Proud parents Barbra Streisand and Elliott Gould pose with their 2-week-old son Jason Gould.

Despite receiving a terrorist threat, Streisand goes on with her one-woman show at a free 1967 Central Park concert given before a crowd of more than 100,000.

12-ounce son arrived, he was beautiful and healthy. His delighted father told the press that although the baby's cleft chin and dark hair resembled his, Jason had his mother's sparkling blue eyes. Elliott and Barbra were proud parents who expected the birth of their son to have a stabilizing effect on their marriage.

Barbra relished her role as mother and fantasized about staying home to care for Jason every day. She even considered having more children, but reality intervened. Columbia Pictures had signed her for the film version of *Funny Girl* a week before Jason's birth, so after a brief four-month respite, Barbra prepared to leave for California. But first, she taped her third television special, "The Belle of 14th Street," in April 1967. A nostalgic show set in the world of vaudeville, it was not as successful as her previous network specials. In May she flew to Hollywood to begin rehearsals for the musical numbers in *Funny Girl*, which would start filming that summer. On the set, Barbra quickly won the admiration and respect of her peers. She not only arrived promptly and put in long hours each day but also showed an inquisitive enthusiasm about all aspects of filmmaking, particularly the techniques used to record her songs.

On June 16, 1967, Streisand left Hollywood and flew back to New York for a free concert she was giving the next day in Central Park. There had been heavy advance publicity for the event, which was also being filmed as a special for CBS. Yet even Barbra was not prepared for the enormous crowd of 135,000 people who greeted her at showtime. Wearing a filmy chiffon gown and an elegant upswept hairdo, she commented on what a beautiful night it was. Then she began singing the songs that had made her famous, "People," "Second Hand Rose," and "Happy Days Are Here Again." When the two-and-a-half hour program ended, Barbra had sung 36 songs to an adoring audience.

Outwardly the evening had been another big success, but it also had a dark side for Barbra. Unknown to anyone but herself and a few others, she had received a death threat from the Palestine Liberation Organization (PLO) shortly before the performance began. Delaying her appearance for 45 minutes, she had seriously considered a last-minute cancellation. Although she finally decided to go on, she was experiencing so much terror despite her self-assured façade that she forgot the lyrics to one of her songs. That evening marked the beginning of a struggle with chronic stage fright that would last 27 long years.

One of the earliest publicity photos of Barbra Streisand, for the movie version of Funny Girl.

5

HELLO, HOLLYWOOD

While Barbra still continued recording albums for Columbia Records, which released *Simply Streisand* and the more successful *A Christmas Album* in 1967, her music now took a backseat to filmmaking. Working with legendary Hollywood director William Wyler, she concentrated on making her screen portrayal of Fanny Brice in *Funny Girl* even more accomplished than her stage performance in the role. Having already conquered Broadway, she was now determined to show Hollywood that she was its new superstar.

In September 1967 the four-month-long filming of *Funny Girl* began. Omar Sharif, a charismatic, dark-eyed Egyptian actor who had scored a triumph in the movie *Dr. Zhivago*, was cast opposite Barbra in the role of Nicky Arnstein. According to Sharif, he and Barbra fell in love while making the movie, but Barbra's public statements about Sharif have never confirmed an affair between them. Still, the rumors in the press about their supposed relationship put a strain on her marriage with Elliott Gould. He tried to defend his wife as "a terribly naïve girl from Brooklyn," adding "I love and trust her all the way."

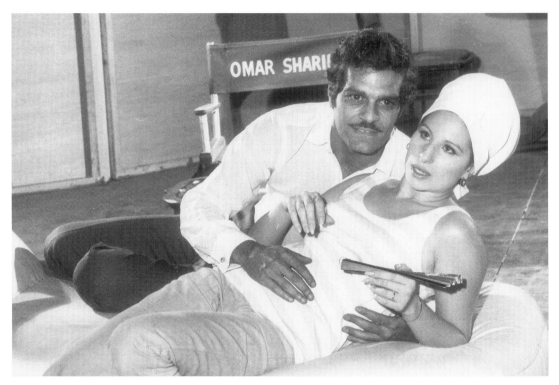

Barbra Streisand rehearses for her first motion picture, Funny Girl, *with costar Omar Sharif. Rumors of a relationship between the two stars would threaten Barbra's marriage.*

Barbra and director William Wyler worked well together once he adjusted to her voracious curiosity about the entire process of film production. Because Barbra knew the role of Fanny Brice so well and because she wanted her screen debut to be successful, she obsessed over minute details of the movie's lighting, camera operation, makeup, and wardrobe. Wyler remained calm and allowed Barbra to put most of her ideas into action because he understood that they both wanted only the best. "I couldn't have wanted a better relationship," Barbra said of her rapport with Wyler, and Wyler dismissed sporadic reports in the media that Barbra was being difficult and domineering on the set. "She's no more difficult than any other actor or actress who's an artist," he said.

By the time the filming of *Funny Girl* ended in December 1967, Barbra had begun feuding with the producer, Ray Stark, who insisted that she fulfill her four-picture contract with his company, Rastar. Barbra had wanted to do only *Funny Girl* for Stark, but she finally relented and the dispute was settled out of court. Yet the disagreement left her dreaming of the day she would control her own destiny not only as an actress but also as a filmmaker.

Around this time, Barbra read "Yentl, the Yeshiva Boy," a short story by Isaac Bashevis Singer about a girl who pretended to be a boy so that she could study the Talmud. When she suggested to her manager, Marty Erlichman, that the story would make a wonderful movie, he—as well as several other people to whom she showed the story—disagreed. But Barbra trusted her own intuition: in January 1968 she bought the film rights to the story, promising herself that someday she would make it into a film.

In April 1968, Barbra began working on a new movie, the film version of Broadway's *Hello Dolly!* The role of matchmaker Dolly Levy was a part originally written for an older, more matronly woman. In taking it on, Barbra faced resentment from the Hollywood community because sentimental favorite Carol Channing was not chosen to recreate the role she had made famous on Broadway. Once again, Barbra was in the position of being an outsider who had to prove her opponents wrong. She also had to prove to the cast and to director Gene Kelly that she was not as temperamental as the media had reported during the filming of *Funny Girl*.

Despite some loud disagreements on the set with her costar, Walter Matthau, who felt she was overly aggressive in making suggestions about production matters, Barbra won the admiration of director Kelly. "Barbra wouldn't do anything to anyone deliberately," said Kelly. "Whatever Walter claims she did, like stepping on his lines or telling him what to do was done out of sheer ignorance or insecurity. She's not that kind of person."

Five months later, when the movie's filming finally

ended, Barbra, Kelly, and the cast were relieved, for it had been a costly, time-consuming, and emotionally difficult production. But Barbra had the satisfaction of having been paid generously—close to a million dollars—for her portrayal of Dolly, as well as the validation that came from seeing most of her creative suggestions about production implemented despite Matthau's objections.

On September 18, 1968, Barbra attended the premier of *Funny Girl* at the Criterion Theatre in New York. She wore an elegant cape and gown as she walked with Elliott down a red carpet lined with admiring fans. After the premiere, there was a party across the street from the theater in a tent set up right in the middle of Times Square just for the occasion. The atmosphere was upbeat and festive, for the first reviews were already out, and they were overwhelmingly favorable. Rex Reed wrote that Streisand's performance was "the most remarkable screen debut I will probably ever see in my lifetime." It was clear that Barbra had scored another triumph. The soundtrack of the movie *Funny Girl* peaked at number 12 on *Billboard*'s chart, where it remained for 108 weeks, a new record for any Streisand album.

In October 1968, Barbra went into rehearsal for her third film, *On A Clear Day You Can See Forever,* based on a mid-1960s Broadway show about a college girl, Daisy Gamble, who discovers past lives while under hypnosis by a psychiatrist who is trying to cure her of smoking. French actor Yves Montand was selected for the role of the psychiatrist in a cast that included fledgling comic Bob Newhart and the relatively unknown Jack Nicholson, who had a minor role as Daisy's brother.

Directed by Vincente Minnelli, the filming of *Clear Day*, which began in January 1969, went smoothly. Barbra had a good rapport with Minnelli, whom she respected, and although she was not overly fond of Montand, they were courteous and professional with each other on the set. When the film was released, reviewers criticized Montand's acting as awkward and detached, but they were entranced by Barbra's vibrant performance as Daisy. Although not an overwhelming box-office success, the movie did break even; the soundtrack album would prove Barbra's least successful.

Meanwhile, in a cruel parallel to the story of Fanny Brice and her husband, Nicky Arnstein, the marriage of Barbra Streisand and Elliott Gould had begun to falter. Like Fanny's, Barbra's career had taken off while her husband's career had not really gotten started. The result was that Barbra supported them, which hurt Elliott's pride. "I never envisioned myself living with someone so rich, so powerful, so famous," Gould later commented. "To have a relationship with someone as successful as Barbra made it difficult

Nineteen-month-old Jason Gould visits his mother on the set of Barbra's second film, Hello Dolly, *a musical comedy based on the Broadway show.*

for me to face myself or find myself." In February 1969 the couple sadly announced their separation, although their divorce was not finalized until 1971. Elliott later went on to become a star in his own right in the movies *Bob and Carol and Ted and Alice*, *M*A*S*H*, and *The Long Goodbye*. Barbra and Elliott Gould would remain devoted parents to their son, Jason.

Despite their formal separation, it was Elliott who escorted Barbra to the Academy Awards on the night of April 14, 1969. Her nomination for Best Actress of 1968 for her performance in *Funny Girl* had thrilled her, but also left her dazed with nervous tension. Clad

in a black transparent outfit designed by Arnold Scaasi for her role in *Clear Day*, Barbra heard a tie announced between herself and Katherine Hepburn. "It's you!" said Elliott. Barbra somehow managed to make her way to the podium, tripping and almost tearing her filmy pant leg on the way. "Hello, gorgeous!" she said to her new Oscar statuette, echoing her opening line in *Funny Girl*. She went on to give a witty, gracious acceptance speech: "Somebody once said to me, asked me if I was happy and I said, 'Are you kidding? I'd be miserable if I was happy.' And I'd like to thank all the members of the Academy for making me *really* miserable." The Oscar validated Barbra's acting talent in a way that no other award could. She finally felt welcomed into the inner sanctum of the Hollywood film industry.

Now that her film career had taken an upswing, Barbra wanted her recording career to catch up, for it had recently lost some of its original momentum. After completing a four-week engagement at the International Hotel in Las Vegas in July 1969, she reviewed a videotape of her performance. She then decided the time had come to update her public image and her music. She wanted to shed the elaborate designer gowns and wigs for a more simple, youthful look. She was only 28 years old, but her dramatic diva outfits made her seem much older. Her music also needed to change. Her most recent album, *What About Today?* (released in 1969), had made a halfhearted attempt to reach out to younger listeners with songs by Paul Simon, John Lennon, and Paul McCartney, but it had not appealed to record buyers. She was now ready to enter the field of pop music more decisively.

Two albums from 1971, *Stoney End* and *Barbra Joan Streisand*, showed definite progress in this direction. "Stoney End" later became a hit single, her first since "People" to land in the Top 10. When she returned to Las Vegas the following year, she used material from both of her new hit albums, and she presented a more hip physical image, wearing tailored pantsuits and a long, straight hairdo.

Barbra had also recently made a new film, *The Owl and the Pussycat*, which was a decisive shift from her three earlier movies because it was nonmusical. By accepting the role of Doris the hooker, she hoped to prove that she still had box-office clout when she simply acted and did not sing. The comedy, based on a London stage play, starred George Segal as Barbra's romantic lead. Although the on-screen chemistry with her two former leading men, Walter Matthau and Yves Montand, had not struck sparks, her connection with Segal was electric. "I think there's Brando and there's Barbra," said Segal. "She has an unerring instinct; she's a natural phenomena." When it opened in November

1970, *The Owl and the Pussycat* was a big hit that helped Barbra change the direction of her film career. Her success in this nonmusical romantic comedy meant that she would not be restricted only to singing roles.

From November 27, 1970, through January 2, 1971, Barbra was back in Las Vegas performing concert engagements at the Riviera and the Hilton International. Although she still disliked performing live, she was obligated to fulfill earlier contracts with both hotels.

That spring, reports surfaced in the press of a budding romance between Barbra and actor Ryan O'Neal, who was her romantic lead in a new comedy, *What's Up, Doc?* The movie would begin filming that summer under the direction of Peter Bogdanovich. Barbra now had a new "California girl" look. Her skin was tanned, her hair long and blonde, and her body toned and voluptuous. When she was photographed with the handsome, sexy O'Neal, whom she had begun dating that spring, they seemed like the classic Hollywood couple.

Because neither Ryan nor Barbra were experienced with the kind of zany, slapstick comedy that Bogdanovich had in mind, they both struggled with feelings of insecurity and doubt during the making of the film. "Every day was hard," O'Neal recalled. "I would go in with butterflies in my stomach." Barbra's anxiety was even worse, and she repeatedly told Bogdanovich that she did not think the film was funny. For once, however, her intuition failed her. *What's Up, Doc?* was a smash hit when it was released the following spring. Not only did the public find the film's 1930s-style screwball humor funny, but they were also charmed by the romantic chemistry between O'Neal and Streisand, which was surely helped by their offscreen relationship.

Shortly after the opening of *What's Up, Doc?* Barbra appeared in a benefit concert in Los Angeles for George McGovern, who was running against Richard Nixon

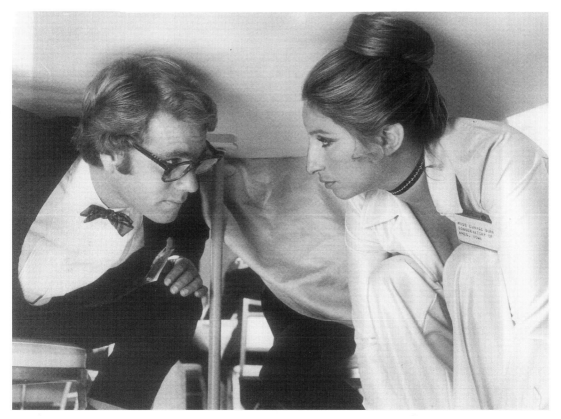

for president. On April 15, 1972, some 20,000 people jammed the Los Angeles Forum to hear Barbra, Carole King, and James Taylor sing. Once again, Barbra was tense about the live concert, but she also worried that her image was not current enough to interest the youthful crowd. At the last minute, she decided to include her pop hit, "Stoney End," persuading Richard Perry, who produced the album of the concert, to write the lyrics of the song on the floor of the stage so she would not forget them. Barbra's performance was a sensation and earned her a Grammy nomination for Best Female Pop Vocal Performance. The event raised $300,000 and marked Barbra's entrance into the arena of political activism. She met with McGovern after the concert to express her views on a number of issues that troubled her, including the Vietnam War and the

Clowning around with costar Ryan O'Neal in the 1972 slapstick comedy What's Up, Doc?

ongoing struggle for women's rights. But her primary concern was still filmmaking. It would be a decade before she took part in another political fund-raiser.

Having succeeded in a romantic comedy, Barbra now needed a new screen challenge. She found it in *Up the Sandbox*, a film based on a novel by Anne Roiphe that started shooting in Los Angeles in March 1972. This story of a young Manhattan housewife's conflicting desires to stay home and to make her mark in the world had captured Barbra's imagination. She was especially intrigued by the fantasy sequences in which the housewife, Margaret Reynolds, challenges Fidel Castro at a news conference, plots with black revolutionaries to destroy the Statue of Liberty, and travels to Africa. "Fantasies can make a rich inner life," she said. "They can lead you places. If I never had a fantasy about being an actress, perhaps I wouldn't have become one." Barbra felt that the film made an important statement about the predicament of American women. As usual, Barbra savored being the outsider who took a position that questioned the more conventional way of thinking. Although critics praised her performance, the film was not a commercial success.

But Barbra's next movie more than made up for the financial failure of *Up the Sandbox*. *The Way We Were*, which began filming in New York in September 1972, restored her status as a screen star with major box-office appeal. Just as the role of Fanny Brice was a perfect match for Barbra's madcap personality, the part of the independent-minded liberal, Katie Morosky, was one that seemed custom-made for her as well. When Robert Redford was cast as the cool, good-looking, and aloof Hubbell Gardiner, director Sydney Pollack and producer Ray Stark began to feel that the movie would be a hit.

A classic love story, *The Way We Were* succeeded because of the dramatic contrast between the detached Redford and the impassioned Streisand. Their pairing proved to be a stroke of casting genius that helped to make the movie one of the top films of 1973. And its title song, sung by Barbra, went straight to the top of the *Billboard* chart. It would go on to win not only the Oscar for Best Song but also the Grammy for Song of the Year. *The Way We Were* is one Streisand film that seems to gain in popularity with the passing of years. Today both the film and the song remain timeless romantic classics.

During a one-week period in May 1973, Barbra made the television special "Barbra Streisand . . . and Other Musical Instruments." But the program did not create the sensation that Barbra's first two specials had. It was freighted with elaborate musical numbers, ornate costumes and props, and a dizzying array of exotic musical instruments. The music consisted of standard Broadway show tunes and only a passing nod to the more contemporary sound of her recent albums. Although Barbra's poignant duet with Ray Charles was easily the highlight of the show, the song was not enough to ensure good reviews. Critics denounced the show as overproduced, although it fared well in the ratings and even went on to win five Emmy Awards.

When Barbra's contract with CBS expired the following year, she did not renew it. She wanted to devote more time to her movie career, but she also needed more time for her personal life. A new man had entered her life, one who would strongly influence it and her career for years to come.

The Way We Were, *starring Barbra Streisand and Robert Redford, affirmed her box-office appeal after the financial failure of* Up the Sandbox. *Both the single "The Way We Were" and the movie album were number one hits.*

Barbra holds her two 1984 Golden Globe Awards for Best Director and for Best Picture. With the movie Yentl, *Streisand accomplished a triple play: she was a successful singer, actress, and filmmaker.*

6

TRIPLE PLAY

On a hot day in August 1973, famed hairdresser Jon Peters waited impatiently in a downstairs room of Barbra Streisand's Beverly Hills mansion. She had made an appointment to see him but had kept him waiting for an hour and a half. When she finally appeared, he was angry. She wanted him to design a wig for her new movie, *For Pete's Sake*. He brusquely replied that he did not do wigs and that he did not like to be kept waiting. Barbra was startled by his brash manner and strong ego. But secretly, she admired him.

Meeting Jon Peters was like meeting a male counterpart to herself. Like her, he had led a life of change. He had gone to reform school as a boy, worked as an extra in movies, traveled in Europe, and had even been an amateur boxer. Although he was now a sought-after hair stylist who owned three upscale salons in Los Angeles, he had begun feeling restless and in need of a new challenge when he met Barbra. The two quickly fell in love. The following month, when shooting of *For Pete's Sake* began, Peters was part of the entourage that came to Manhattan with Barbra. He had sold his salons to devote himself entirely to her career.

Making the frothy movie comedy proved a lark for Barbra and her male costar, a gentle, sensitive actor named Michael Sarrazin. Barbra's exuberant portrayal of a wife who gets involved with the Mafia when she tries to help her mild-mannered husband had far less substance than her previous film roles, but she was too happy to care. She was back home in New York City, and she was with Peters, the love of her life. Although *For Pete's Sake* was no blockbuster, it did not tarnish Barbra's reputation as an actress. By now Barbra had a strong following of fans who would attend any movie she was in.

As Barbra became more deeply involved with Peters, she began reinventing her image according to his idealized vision of her. When he suggested that she lose weight during the filming of *For Pete's Sake*, she agreed. She also consented to a new, shorter hairdo. Jon wanted her to try different things in both her personal and professional life. Envisioning a more sexy and youthful Barbra, he set about looking for the projects that would allow this new image of her to emerge.

Ray Stark's new film, *Funny Lady*, was not the project Jon or Barbra had in mind. The sequel to *Funny Girl* was the final film in Barbra's four-picture commitment to Stark. At first Barbra flatly refused to make the movie because she wanted to leave the Fanny Brice story behind for good and start making her own films. She believed in Jon's daring vision of her, and agreed with him that portraying an aging vaudeville actress was not the way to achieve a sexier public image.

Still, Streisand was anxious to end her obligation to Stark, so she braced herself and began working on the picture in the spring of 1974. She did at least enjoy spending time with her costar, James Caan, whose feistiness matched her own. "I liked her despite the stories the tabloids tried to spread," Caan later said. "She's an interesting and ambitious woman—there should be more ladies like that in the world." But like most

sequels, *Funny Lady* never recaptured the spark of the original. Although critics found much to admire in Barbra's acting and singing in the movie, they felt that *Funny Girl* was better.

ButterFly, an album that began production during the shooting of *Funny Lady*, marked the debut of Jon Peters into the music world. The inspiration for the album's title was a shimmering diamond and sapphire butterfly that Peters had given Barbra as a gift. He had also told her that she reminded him of a butterfly when they first met, so the image had romantic meaning for them as a couple. It was Barbra's bravest and most experimental album, bringing together pop, gospel-soul, reggae, and country music. Jon's concept for the album cover was bolder still: a fly poised on a stick of butter. Some critics agreed with Barbra, who stated *ButterFly* contained some of her best singing ever, but

Boyfriend Jon Peters devoted himself to Barbra's career, helping her reinvent her image in both film and musical directions.

Although critics panned the 1976 remake of A Star Is Born, *which stars Barbra Streisand and Kris Kristofferson as rock singers, the film swept the Golden Globe Awards the following year. The movie ultimately became Barbra's most financially successful.*

others found weaknesses. The *Los Angeles Times* said her voice was still beautiful, but that she had "no clear feel for interpreting contemporary pop music." The public liked the recording well enough, however, to make it one of her gold albums.

While Jon Peters withdrew from musical production to concentrate on Barbra's film career, Barbra sought a new collaborator for her next pop album, *Lazy Afternoon*. She finally settled on singer/songwriter Rupert Holmes, whose songs on his *Widescreen* album had won her admiration. When her office called, asking him to leave New York and come to Los Angeles to produce her new album, he was flabbergasted, but he quickly agreed. Holmes and Streisand worked well together because they admired each other's work and understood each other's style. In April 1975 they began recording *Lazy Afternoon*, finishing three months later. Holmes felt he had been successful in creating a sound for Barbra that was traditional, yet not dated. "Someone like Barbra will always sound modern," he said. "Barbra doesn't need disco or new wave to be modern. Barbra is Barbra."

Jon Peters believed in Barbra and felt she would succeed in any new project she chose. He was her enthusiastic collaborator when she announced her plan to produce and star in a musical remake of *A Star Is Born*, a 1937 film that had also been remade in 1954,

starring Judy Garland and James Mason. After seven
different rewrites on the script and a long search for
the leading man, the movie began shooting in February 1976. Kris Kristofferson was Barbra's costar,
Barbra was star and executive producer, and Jon Peters
was producer. The film's plot bore a strong similarity
to Barbra's relationship with Elliott Gould: an actor's
career disintegrates while his aspiring-actress girl-
friend's takes flight. In the new remake, the actor and
actress were now rock singers, and their relationship in
some ways reflected the volatile nature of the romance
between Streisand and Peters.

The boiling point of what proved to be a stressful
production was the filming of a live rock concert scene
at Sun Devil Stadium in Arizona. Barbra, Jon, and Kris
had an onstage argument that was audible to the
70,000 assembled fans and members of the press.
Streisand was heard swearing at Kristofferson, who
swore back at her. Peters angrily intervened, challenging Kristofferson to a fight after the filming was over.
Yet when the time came for Barbra to sing, the crowd
still found her performance compelling. After singing
"People" and "The Way We Were," she concluded with
a new song, "Evergreen," which she and Paul Williams
had written for the film. The crowd's applause thun-
dered, thrilling Barbra. "I'm really glad you like it," she
said, "because that's the first time I ever sang that song
in front of people."

When the movie opened on December 18, 1976, it
was savagely attacked by the critics. Rex Reed said it
was "the worst movie of 1976," and Janet Maslin of
Newsweek said the film was "almost as self-destructive
as its suicidal leading man." But Barbra and Jon Peters
had the satisfaction of seeing their film sweep the
Golden Globe Awards in 1977; it also went on to
become the most financially successful movie musical
ever made. And the tenderly lyrical ballad "Evergreen"
won an Oscar for its composers, Barbra Streisand and

Above: The love song "Evergreen" from A Star Is Born *won a Golden Globe for Best Song, presented by actor Michael Douglas (left) to cocomposers Barbra Streisand and Paul Williams. Right: The song also earned Streisand two Grammys for Best Female Vocal and for Song of the Year.*

Paul Williams at the 1977 Academy Awards. Barbra was overjoyed as she accepted her award. "Never in my wildest dreams did I ever imagine I'd win an Oscar for writing a song," she gushed. "I'm very excited and very grateful."

For Barbra, *A Star Is Born* was an important break-through in her career. As the film's star and executive producer, she had feared that her reputation as both an actress and a filmmaker was on the line. There had been so much negative publicity surrounding the movie before its release that Barbra, despite Jon's help and support, had begun to worry that *A Star Is Born* might be the last film she would ever make. But those who doubted the film's success beforehand had over-looked one important point: it had a soundtrack filled with songs sung by Barbra Streisand.

With the popularity of the song "Evergreen," both the movie and the recorded soundtrack were hugely profitable. The fierce media attacks on the production partnership between Streisand and Peters melted into a vapor as ticket sales soared in America and abroad. Barbra had triumphed again financially, but, more important, she had won the respect of the industry as a filmmaker who could make hit movies.

In the summer of 1977, Barbra's album *Streisand Superman* was released. It sealed her artistry as a pop performer, with a single from the album, "My Heart Belongs to Me," shooting to the top of the charts. The album cover also created a sensation, for it embodied the look that Jon Peters had in mind when he first met Barbra. Wearing sexy white short-shorts, knee socks, and a tight T-shirt, she raised her fist in the power salute that had become the emblematic gesture of the women's liberation movement. A woman can be sexy and strong, the photograph seemed to suggest. *Playboy* magazine was so taken with Barbra's *Superman* outfit that its editors asked her to wear it for one of their cov-ers. She agreed, and playfully removed her sneakers and socks for the photo shoot, joking, "Now you can say I took it off for *Playboy!*"

On May 8, 1978, Barbra appeared in a benefit concert honoring Israel's 30th anniversary, joining celebrities like Barry Manilow, Carol Burnett, Paul Newman, Ben Vereen, and Sammy Davis Jr. During the final act of the evening, Barbra appeared onstage wearing a form-fitting white antique lace gown. She sang her own vibrant rendition of "Tomorrow" from the Broadway show *Annie*, as well as favorites like "Happy Days" and "People." After leading the audience through the Israeli national anthem in Hebrew, Barbra conducted a phone/video interview with Israel's former prime minister, Golda Meir, a woman whose courage Barbra had long admired.

A few weeks later, Barbra's hit album *Songbird* was released. It included a song from one of Neil Diamond's albums, "You Don't Bring Me Flowers," which each had recorded as a solo. When a disc jockey in Louisville, Kentucky, realized that both singers had recorded the same single, he decided to mix the songs together so they sounded like a duet. When it aired, the recording caused such a flurry of requests that news of the incident eventually reached Streisand and Diamond, who then recorded a real duet of "You Don't Bring Me Flowers" several months later. The song became the biggest hit of both singers' careers. Interestingly the two had been classmates at Erasmus Hall High School in Brooklyn.

In October 1978, Barbra started shooting *The Main Event* with her former boyfriend Ryan O'Neal. Another breezy comedy, it told the story of Hillary Kramer, the hard-driving president of a perfume company who goes bankrupt and discovers that her only remaining asset is an inept boxer. Hoping to make some money, she attempts to retrain him into a winning prizefighter but falls in love with him instead. For Barbra and O'Neal, the film was a lighthearted romp, but critics found both

the plot and the lead performances rather superficial. The movie was a big winner at the box office, though, because Barbra's fans were thrilled by her on-screen reunion with O'Neal. Audiences also liked the jazzy, disco-style theme song, which was combined with a second song, "Fight," written by Paul Jabara and Bruce Roberts. The pulsing melody established Barbra as a hot new disco singer and paved the way for "Enough Is Enough," a duet with Donna Summer that later became a hit single.

Although *The Main Event* was a big moneymaker for Barbra, it did not contribute to her development as an

At the May 8, 1978, celebration of Israel's 30th anniversary, Barbra Streisand (left) talks with Israel's prime minister, Golda Meir (on screen), via a satellite phone call.

actress or filmmaker. What she needed was a movie that would bring together her singing, acting, and film-making talents in a brilliant, unforgettable way. For years she had continued to believe she had found such a project in "Yentl, the Yeshiva Boy," which she still hoped to turn into a film, despite the fact that most major Hollywood studios had turned down the project.

Two events helped to convince Barbra that the time had come to bring *Yentl* to the screen. In 1979 her brother, Sheldon, took her to visit her father's grave, which she had never seen before. Later, while looking at a picture of her and Sheldon standing beside their father's tombstone, she happened to notice the name "Anschel"—the same name used by Yentl as the Yeshiva Boy—on a nearby tombstone. Stunned, Barbra interpreted this as a sign from her father that she should make the film. A short time later, her brother persuaded her to participate in a séance to try to communicate with her father's spirit. When the message tapped out on the table was "Sorry-sing-proud," a shaken but excited Barbra interpreted this as another sign that *Yentl* should be made.

Yentl was more than Barbra's bid to make a feminist statement or to reaffirm her Jewish heritage: she wanted to resolve her feelings about her dead father. For a long time, she had felt angry and deprived because she had no father. But with the help of psychotherapy, she had confronted childhood fears that she might have caused her father's death by being a bad girl. Now she truly understood that illness alone had caused his death, but he had loved her and been proud of her while he was alive. "I always felt during my life that I had taken on his persona," said Barbra. "I was carrying on my father's life by making something of myself. That's why I dedicated the film to him and to all fathers."

As her effort to launch *Yentl* continued, Barbra took time out in February 1980 to make a new album, *Guilty*, with Barry Gibb of the rock group the Bee

On the set of Yentl. *Nearly 16 years after obtaining film rights for the story, Streisand completed the ambitious project, becoming the first woman in motion picture history to cowrite, direct, produce, and star in a major feature.*

Gees. Gibb was delighted to have the chance to work with Barbra and vowed to make the best Streisand album ever, writing and arranging all the music on the album for her alone. The album sold over 20 million copies. "Guilty," the album's self-titled single, went on to win a Grammy in the Pop Duet category for Streisand and Gibb.

In the summer of 1982 Barbra made what turned out to be her least successful movie, *All Night Long.* Starring Gene Hackman, the film was directed by Jean-Claude Tramont, the husband of Barbra's agent, Sue Mengers. When Tramont decided that actress Lisa Eichhorn was not effective in the role of Cheryl Gibbons, he fired her and hired Barbra for the hefty salary of $4.5 million plus 15 percent of the gross—all for less than a month's work. A subtle, European-style comedy, *All Night Long* never appealed to American audiences or critics. Today even some of Barbra's biggest fans may have forgotten she ever made it.

Barbra persisted in trying to get financial backing for *Yentl*, but she was stonewalled by all the big-name studios, who were convinced that the ethnic focus of the film, its large budget, and Barbra's relative lack of directing experience would preclude its success. A less-determined person might have given up, but Barbra persevered. Finally, on March 31, 1981, United Artists announced that Barbra would cowrite, direct, produce, and star in *Yentl*. Production would begin in February 1982.

The announcement was greeted with surprise and disbelief by the media. How, her doubters wondered, could a woman who was almost 40 portray a 16-year old boy? But an undaunted Barbra only redoubled her efforts on the film, rewriting the script and composing a musical score with Alan and Marilyn Bergman. *Yentl* was the film on which she had staked her money and her reputation. She saw it as the project of a lifetime that would heal her heart, mind, and soul. The feeling that her father was watching over her only strengthened her devotion to making the movie.

The filming of *Yentl* thrust Barbra into the most exhausting work schedule of her life. From the time that shooting for the film's interior scenes began in England on April 14, 1982, until the move to Czechoslovakia for the exterior shots later on, Barbra rose at 5:00 A.M. each morning. She worked all day, and stayed until 2:00 A.M. to make plans for the next day's shooting before going to bed. While the entire cast and crew admired her commitment, drive, and professionalism, they also appreciated her human touch, for she took the time to develop warm personal relationships with every single person on the *Yentl* set—right down to the hairdressers and extras.

For the next seven months, Barbra devoted every waking moment to the movie that had become her obsession. She never got more than three or four hours of sleep a night, but she was too exhilarated by her creative energy and freedom to care. She knew she was finally achieving the kind of artistic control over a film that she had always longed for. "To me, the most creative experience I've ever had was being pregnant," she later said. "This is the second most creative experience: directing a film."

On November 16, 1983, *Yentl* premiered in New York and Los Angeles. Barbra received high praise for all her efforts in the production: performance, singing, and, above all, directing. Unfortunately, one of the few dissenting voices was that of the original story's author, Isaac Bashevis Singer, who disliked the changed ending of the movie, in which Yentl resumes her life as a woman and starts a new life in America. Singer also felt singing to be inappropriate to the film, noting that the character he created did not sing. Yet the overwhelming response to the film was positive. *Yentl* received two Golden Globe Awards for Best Director and Best Picture. It also received five Academy Award nominations, winning for Best Score. A controversy arose over Barbra's exclusion from the categories of acting, direction, screenplay, or production, and a picket line protesting her shutout formed outside the Dorothy Chandler Pavilion on the night of the Academy Awards.

But Barbra took the high road, choosing not to acknowledge any intended slight. She was already secure in her achievement with *Yentl*, which she had starred in, directed, coproduced, and cowritten. For the first time in history, a woman had taken total control of a film. Barbra had now charted a new and exciting course for her future. She was a singer, an actress, and a filmmaker.

A scene from Barbra Streisand's music video Emotion. *When the contemporary pop music approach did not prove successful, Barbra decided her next album would reflect her Broadway musical background.*

7

STREISAND SUPERMAN

For nine years Barbra Streisand had been enthralled by live-in love Jon Peters, but during the filming of *Yentl* their relationship had begun to slowly dissolve. She had to leave Peters and her son, Jason, behind when she went abroad to shoot the film so that she could devote herself completely to the project's success. Although Peters would fly to London and Czechoslovakia from time to time to lend moral support and advice, his commitment to his own career as a producer was deepening. When they finally broke up, Barbra chose to view their long relationship philosophically. "We've separated," she declared. "But I look at it another way: we've lasted nine years. In this town that's an accomplishment." They also dissolved their business partnership, and Marty Erlichman eventually resumed his role as manager of Barbra's career.

Barbra shifted gears and headed back to the recording studio. But the music industry had changed since the making of her last album, *Guilty*. It was now the age of MTV, and a new, visually oriented generation demanded that its music be accompanied by dramatic, fast-paced videos. Barbra's attempted return to pop music, an album with an accompanying video entitled *Emotion*, was released in October 1984 with disappointing results. The single only went to 50th on the *Billboard* chart, while the album reached 19th.

The relatively weak performance of *Emotion* left Barbra wanting to return to her origins—the Broadway show tunes that she had sung with such abandon in her teenaged years and on her early albums. Columbia Records wanted her to try another pop album, but Barbra followed her own inclination. She telephoned composer Stephen Sondheim and asked him to help her adapt three of his songs just for her. She especially wanted him to revise the final lines of the song "Send in the Clowns" from "Well, maybe next year" to "Don't bother; they're here." To her relief, his response was enthusiastic.

Sondheim was an ardent Streisand fan who had long been fascinated by her exceptional talent. "Barbra has one of the two or three best voices in the world of singing songs," he said. "She has the meticulous attention to detail that makes a good artist." He even attended recording sessions so that he could observe firsthand how she worked in the studio. Their artistic merger was as stimulating for Barbra as it was for him. "This was one of the most exciting collaborations I've ever had, because we both talk fast, we think fast; so it was like shorthand half the time . . . we practically didn't have to finish sentences," she said.

In November 1985 *The Broadway Album*, featuring such songs as "Something Wonderful" from *The King and I*, "Somewhere" from *West Side Story*, and "If I Loved You" from *Carousel*, was released. Thanks to a stunning performance in which Barbra maturely balanced heartfelt passion and artistic control, it was the best-selling solo album of her career. Barbra and the album won two Grammys: one for Best Pop Female Vocal Performance and the other for Best Arrangement Accompanying a Vocal. Accepting her eighth Grammy, Barbra observed that it had been exactly 24 years ago that she had won her first Grammy. So popular was the album that a video documentary, *Putting It Together: The Making of "The Broadway Album,"* was shown as a television special on the cable channel Home Box Office (HBO). It later became available as a home video.

From the 1970s to the mid-1980s, Barbra had seldom appeared on the concert stage, concentrating instead on her work in films and recording. She was still fearful of singing in front of live audiences because of the death threat before her 1967 concert in Central Park. The occasion would have to be very special indeed for her to stand up in front of a live audience and sing. But in the spring of 1986, Barbra changed her mind. On April 26, 1986, the nuclear disaster at the Chernobyl power plant in the Soviet Union distressed her so deeply that she decided it was time to overcome her long-standing fear of performing live and use her voice to work for the people and issues she believed in.

Although Streisand had contributed over the years to the campaigns of such Democratic candidates as Edward Kennedy, Birch Bayh of Indiana, and Elizabeth Holtzman of New York, she had not openly endorsed a specific campaign since her concert for McGovern in 1972. Now she began working with Alan and Marilyn Bergman to prepare a private, one-woman fund-raising concert to help get Democratic candidates elected to the Senate in November 1986. The event was called One Voice.

Although lyricist Stephen Sondheim did not usually custom-tailor his songs for performers, when Barbra Streisand requested changes for The Broadway Album, *he agreed. The album includes numbers from* A Little Night Music, West Side Story, Sweeney Todd, *and* Company.

Because 14 years had passed since Barbra's last concert, One Voice quickly became the most sought-after invitation of the Hollywood social season. The September outdoor concert would take place in a specially built amphitheater on the grounds of Streisand's Malibu, California, estate. The invited celebrity guests were asked to donate $2,500 apiece to attend. Not surprisingly, seats for One Voice sold out almost instantaneously. No one wanted to miss the long-awaited return of Barbra Streisand to the concert stage.

On the evening of September 6, 1986, Barbra glided onto the amphitheater stage shrouded in a romantic mist to perform the songs that had made her famous: "People," "Evergreen," "The Way We Were," and numerous others. She gave particularly powerful renditions of "Papa, Can You Hear Me?" from *Yentl* and the song Judy Garland made famous, "Over the Rainbow," which she chose for its hopeful, visionary lyrics. The audience's response surpassed her wildest expectations. One Voice raised $1.5 million in proceeds and established Barbra as one of the most formidable fund-raisers for the Democratic Party in the United States.

In December HBO broadcast the concert as a cable special that promptly became its most requested program. A soundtrack soon followed, and it went platinum. The proceeds from One Voice also enabled Barbra to found and endow the Streisand Foundation, which would give funding to groups promoting environmental protection, women's issues, civil rights, and AIDS research.

In October 1986, Barbra began shooting *Nuts,* her first film in four years. The role of Claudia Draper, a high-priced call girl standing trial for a murder committed in self-defense, presented new challenges to Barbra with its gripping dramatic intensity. She identified closely with the character, who is discovered during an emotional courtroom trial to have been the victim of an abusive stepfather. Richard Dreyfuss was

cast as Claudia's attorney, Maureen Stapleton played her mother, and Karl Malden appeared as the stepfather. Again acting as both producer and star, Barbra went a step further this time and also composed the entire musical score for *Nuts*.

When it was released the following year, in November 1987, *Nuts* got mixed reviews. Although Barbra received raves for her powerful acting, some critics found fault with her for taking on too many tasks for one person to handle in a single production—a criticism that brought an angry response from Barbra. "It's a strange phenomenon that our society is not ready for a Renaissance woman," she reflected. "It is only ready for a Renaissance man. Society still wants to keep women in their place." Although the movie was not a

In the December 1986 cable broadcast of One Voice, a Democratic candidate fund-raising concert that had been taped in September, Barbra gave her first full-length television concert in 20 years.

A short-lived romance with actor Don Johnson resulted in a hit single, "Till I Loved You," the love theme from the unproduced pop opera Goya . . . A Life.

strong performer at the box office, many people still feel that it contains Barbra's strongest acting performance to date.

Barbra's live-in companion since the departure of Jon Peters had been Richard Baskin, who, like Peters, had also shared a professional relationship with her. But after a romance that lasted three years, Streisand and Baskin drifted apart. Over the winter holidays, shortly after the release of *Nuts*, Barbra began dating television star Don Johnson, of *Miami Vice* fame. The couple met during a ski vacation in Aspen, Colorado. Like Peters, Johnson had a checkered past, boyish charm, and a confident—even brash— manner. Barbra and Don made their first appearance as a couple at the Holmes-Tyson boxing match in Atlantic City. The evening was a novel experience for Barbra because it was the first time she was with a man who received more attention from the press than she did.

As their affair became more intense, Barbra and Don ventured into professional collaborations. She appeared in a *Miami Vice* episode broadcast in early 1988, and he joined her in working on a new album, *Till I Loved You*. Although he was not a professional musician, Johnson enjoyed picking out tunes on a guitar and had cowritten songs with Dickie Betts, formerly of the Allman Brothers. Drawing on the electricity of their real-life romance, Barbra and Don recorded the duet "Till I Loved You," a love song from the unproduced musical *Goya*. The single even included a softly lit, romantic picture of them with their arms around each other. Their affair ended shortly before the album's November release, however, and Johnson returned to former wife Melanie Griffith.

Although Barbra's love life may have become unsettled, her work schedule had not, for she had a new project to consume her time and energy. She spent 1989 hard at work on a film adaptation of Pat Conroy's novel *The Prince of Tides*, which she would direct, produce, and star in. From the first time she had read the book, she was attracted to its story of family pain and eventual healing through the process of psychotherapy. She herself had found understanding of her past and a greater sense of control over her future through years of therapy. "The movie is not just about being flawed but about forgiving the flaws in yourself," she said. "Because when you can do that, you can forgive others. How many people love themselves?"

She found her efforts to get financial backing for the movie discouraging until an old friend intervened. Jon Peters, now the cochairman of Columbia Pictures Entertainment, finally pushed the project through. Her work on the movie also brought a new love interest into Barbra's life. James Newton Howard, whom she had hired to compose the music for *The Prince of Tides* after Oscar-winning John Barry quit, became her new companion. "The process of working with her is a difficult one because her perfectionism is unequaled," Howard said. "She's incredibly demanding, but I can truthfully say that working with her has elevated my own work." Once again, Barbra's romantic partner was also a collaborator in her career. Barbra's ability to stay on good terms with old flames has helped her maintain useful professional alliances even after her romances ended.

Barbra wanted to choose exactly the right person for the male lead of *Tides*. Tom Wingo, the southern schoolteacher who tries to help his sister after her

With Nick Nolte in a scene from the 1991 film The Prince of Tides. *It was the second successful film that Streisand directed, produced, and starred in.*

suicide attempt, and is himself helped by a psychiatrist named Susan Lowenstein, was a challenging role that demanded a complex blend of strength and vulnerability. Barbra considered many fine actors—from Warren Beatty to Robert Redford—but she finally settled on Nick Nolte. She had greatly admired his performance in the 1990 Sidney Lumet film *Q & A.*

Streisand cast Blythe Danner as Tom's wife. For the part of his mother— both as a younger and an older woman—she selected Kate Nelligan. But her most controversial choice was for the part of Susan Lowenstein's teenage son: she cast her own son, Jason Gould. He was eager to try the role, and she trusted him to deliver a sincere, heartfelt performance.

Guarding her recording career against a slump, Barbra was also working with Marty Erlichman on a four-CD career retrospective entitled *Just for the Record. . . .* Starting with the very roots of her singing career—a recording of "You'll Never Know" that she had made with her mother during a vacation in the New York Catskills in 1955—she included several other previously unreleased recordings, among them her famous television duet with Judy Garland. For the finish, the seasoned, 49-year-old Barbra harmonized on "You'll Never Know" with the 13-year-old Barbra's more tentative recording of the same song. By the time *The Prince of Tides* was ready to shoot, Barbra had completed her CD retrospective, and its release was scheduled for the fall of the next year.

The Prince of Tides began shooting in Beaufort, South Carolina, in June 1990. Shooting continued later in New York City, where Barbra found a welcome respite from the sweltering southern heat in her air-conditioned Manhattan duplex. She was relieved to be back in her hometown. Production stayed on schedule through late September, when it finally wrapped. Although Columbia Pictures originally wanted to release the movie for Christmas 1990, Barbra's insistence that she be allowed more time to edit the film caused Columbia to postpone its release until the following year.

On December 11, 1991, *The Prince of Tides* finally opened in Los Angeles. Critical response to the movie was overwhelmingly positive. Both Barbra's acting and directing talents received high praise, and Nolte's performance was thought by many to be the finest of his career. Commercially, the movie was one of the most successful films of the year, grossing $75 million.

Not only did the release of *Tides* ensure Barbra's reputation as a director, but its commercial success also meant that she was in complete control as a filmmaker. She could now routinely expect to enjoy the freedom that had always been so important to her artistic development. To Barbra, the freedom to practice her art her way—whether that art was created on a concert stage, on a movie screen, or in an editing room—was what she had always hoped for. "I believe that art is a very living process, that as we grow, our art grows, as we expand, our work expands," she once observed. *The Prince of Tides* gave her the opportunity to express her artistry with new depths of feeling.

Barbra Streisand receives a 1992 Grammy honoring her career achievements. Although many consider her to be a legend in the entertainment field, she responds, "In all honesty, I don't feel like a legend. I feel like a work in progress."

8

A WORK IN PROGRESS

W hen the 1991 Academy Award nominations were announced late in February 1992, shock waves resounded through the motion picture industry. Although *The Prince of Tides* received seven nominations, Barbra's name was mysteriously absent from the list of nominees for Best Director. The omission was especially startling because just a few weeks earlier she had been honored as one of five directors—and the third woman ever—to be nominated for the Directors Guild of America prize.

Her snub by the Academy renewed controversy over sexism in the filmmaking industry. In a speech that Barbra delivered a few months later to the organization Women in Film, she boldly spoke out against gender discrimination in Hollywood. "If a man wants to get it right, he's looked up to and respected," she said. "If a woman wants to get it right, she's difficult and impossible." Ironically, Barbra's exclusion from the Academy Award nominees for direction generated fresh publicity for *The Prince of Tides* and increased its box-office take.

Barbra now returned to the concert stage. On September 16, 1992, she sang in a fund-raiser for the Democratic presidential ticket of Bill Clinton–Al Gore at the Ted Field estate in California. The very mention of Streisand's name in the program made the evening a sellout. Two months later when she received the AIDS Project Los Angeles Commitment to Life Award, she again appeared onstage, this time with Johnny Mathis to sing two duets from *West Side Story*, "I Have A Love"/"One Hand, One Heart" and "Somewhere."

But Barbra's largest audience came after Clinton's presidential victory in November when she agreed to sing at the inaugural festivities. On January 19, 1993, wearing a seductive three-piece suit slit to the thigh, she once again charmed audiences with some of her best-known songs. Although other stars appeared in the program with her, including Michael Jackson, Aretha Franklin, and Fleetwood Mac, only Barbra's performance was broadcast in its entirety as a CBS television special, and it was Barbra who introduced President Clinton to the audience.

Barbra's romantic life had downshifted since her breakup with Jon Peters. While she was intermittently linked with tennis player Andre Agassi, whose matches she attended in the fall of 1992 and again in June of 1993, there was no new steady man in her life. She continued to be seen in public occasionally with Richard Baskin, but both Streisand and Baskin insisted that they were just good friends. The true nature of her bonds with these men remains a mystery—and Barbra seems to prefer it that way.

At the end of 1992, Barbra negotiated a $60 million contract with Sony, including $2 million a year for 10 years to develop film projects and $5 million each for six albums. Her first new album for Sony confirmed the company's belief in her enduring popularity. *Back to Broadway*, her 50th album, was released in June 1993. It debuted on the *Billboard* album chart at number one.

One of the secrets to Barbra's remarkable success is her capacity to surprise people. Just when the public feels it can predict the course of her career, she makes a completely unexpected move. Although she had developed a very bad case of stage fright after her concert in Central Park in 1967, Barbra had in fact been ambivalent about live performance even before being threatened. "I have a mixture of feelings about performing live," she remarked. "In the beginning, I guess I enjoyed concerts as a forum for expressing myself. . . . But truthfully, I would rather do something in private, like a movie or a record and then share it with an audience when I am done."

But in the fall of 1993, Barbra made an electrifying announcement. After an absence of 27 years from the public concert stage, she had decided to return. She would give two concerts at the new MGM Grand Hotel in Las Vegas, one on New Year's Eve and one on New Year's Day. The public responded first with disbelief—then with a frantic scramble for tickets. Despite hefty prices for seats, which ranged from $500 to $1,000, the concerts sold out almost immediately.

The spectacular success of the two MGM Grand Hotel shows brought another momentous announcement from Barbra. In March 1994 she revealed that she had decided to do a 12-stop concert tour. When asked to comment on her change of heart about performing live, she answered, "I honestly believed it was going to be just two concerts. But it was such a lovely experience—feeling the connection with the audience after all these years—that I decided to do a limited tour to

Barbra Streisand introduces President-elect Bill Clinton to the crowd at the Presidential Gala held at the Capital Centre in Landover, Maryland, the night before his 1993 inauguration.

A fan sporting a Streisand sweatshirt holds one of her $1,000 tickets for the 1994 New Year's Day concert at the MGM Grand Hotel, in Las Vegas. Six years later, tickets for the millennium New Year's performances would range from $500 to $2,500.

express my admiration for the love and support I have received for such a long time." She scheduled stops in such cities as New York, London, Anaheim, San Francisco, Washington, D.C., and Detroit, but wound up doubling the number of scheduled shows because of an overwhelming demand for tickets, which sold out in each city within an hour of going on sale. Wherever she performed, Barbra broke all previous box-office records: by the tour's conclusion she had grossed around $70 million. Over $10.25 million went to charities that Barbra supports.

Her comeback show began with an adaptation of "As If We Never Said Good-bye," which she sang while slowly descending a staircase. It was an emotional moment, and by the time she finished the final line, "I've come home again," her audience burst into wild applause. Next she shifted to the playfully confident

"I'm Still Here," a wry commentary on her enduring achievements in fields she had once been discouraged from entering, such as songwriting, acting, producing, and directing. Between songs, she smoothed her sleek pageboy hairdo and occasionally paused to sip a cup of tea. She sang "Can't Help Lovin' That Man" seated and wistfully harmonized "I'll Know When My Love Comes Along" with the image of a youthful Marlon Brando on video. The show took on a distinctly melancholy tone when she recalled the heartbreaks of her own adolescence with such songs as "People" and "Lover Man, Where Can You Be?" She echoed the inherent difficulties of all male-female relationships in thrilling renditions of "Will He Like Me?" "He Touched Me," "Evergreen," and "The Man Who Got Away." Punctuating the songs with remarks that were sometimes philosophic, she created a program that was not just a concert but also a personal memoir in song.

For the second half of the program, Barbra changed from her black velvet gown into a floor-length, beaded white suit and vest. She continued with romantic hits like "The Way We Were" and "You Don't Bring Me Flowers." During her performance in New York's Madison Square Garden, which her son, Jason, attended, she sang "Nothing's Going to Harm You" to him. In a moving gesture at the song's end, she silently mouthed, "I love you," to which he replied, "I love you too." She offered a strong, heartfelt version of "Papa, Can You Hear Me?" from *Yentl*, and concluded with her famous "Happy Days Are Here Again," which she presented as a ringing affirmation of her support for President Clinton's policies.

Barbra's majestic concert performance received admiring reviews from the critics. *New York Times* music critic Stephen Holden likened her to "an exiled queen returning to claim her throne." He praised her enduring status as a pop music diva, noting that her remarkable talent was enhanced by an unusual romantic sensitivity and a powerful will. "What elevates Ms. Streisand above her imitators," he wrote, "is a dramatic instinct that turns everything into a continually unfolding expression of feeling."

When "Barbra: The Concert" was presented as a cable special on HBO on August 21, 1994, it received the highest ratings of any original entertainment special in HBO history. In September 1994, Columbia Records released a multidisc recording of *Barbra: The Concert*, her 51st album. Both the CD and the video, released in December 1994, are highly polished presentations in which all technical details, such as sound and lighting, were personally supervised by Streisand. She won two Emmys as star and producer of the video program. Yet the most important achievement of the concert tour for Barbra was not financial but personal, for she had overcome her stage fright. She had also proved to the world that she could still stir audiences with her powerful singing voice.

For almost four decades Barbra Streisand has beguiled the American public with her romantic singing, her vibrant acting, and her inventively conceived and directed films. But her accomplishments transcend the world of show business. She has been a spokesperson for women's issues and a political activist who has spoken out for such diverse causes as welfare reform, human and civil rights, and federal support for the arts. A vocal defender of civil liberties, Streisand appeared at Harvard University's John F. Kennedy School of Government on February 3, 1995, to present a speech entitled, "The Artist as Citizen." Her address received extensive print and television coverage.

Barbra's company, Barwood Productions, produces movies that examine social, historical, and political issues. In the spring of 1995, NBC Television aired *Serving in Silence: The Margarethe Cammermeyer Story*. The film, directed by Streisand and starring Glenn Close, investigates the repression of civil rights for gays

"The Artist as Citizen"

Excerpts from the speech given by Barbra Streisand to the John F. Kennedy School of Government, Harvard University, Cambridge Massachusetts, on February 3, 1995:

The subject of my talk is the artist as citizen. I guess I can call myself an artist, although after thirty years, the word still feels a bit pretentious. But I am, first and foremost, a citizen: a tax-paying, voting, concerned American citizen who happens to have opinions. . . .

After many years of self-scrutiny, I've realized that the most satisfying feelings come from things outside myself. And I believe that people from any walk of life when they stand up for their convictions can do almost anything—stop wars, end injustices, and even defeat entrenched powers. . . .

We . . . need to keep in mind some words spoken by the man for whom this school of government is named. President Kennedy said he valued so much what artists could give because they "knew the midnight as well as the high noon [and] understood the ordeal as well as the triumph of the human spirit.". . . Well aware that art can be controversial, he concluded, "[the artist] must often sail against the currents of his time. This is not a popular role."

But in 1995, I continue to believe it is an indispensable one—that artists, especially those who have had success, and have won popularity in their work, not only have the right, but the responsibility, to risk the unpopularity of being committed and active.

We receive so much from our country; we can and should give something back.

in the military. The movie won three Emmys, six Emmy nominations, and the Peabody Award. A 1998 television movie produced by Barwood, *The Long Island Incident: The Caroline McCarthy Story*, tells the true story of a wife and mother-turned-gun control activist. *Rescuers: Stories of Courage* was a 1997-98 series of six dramas shown on the cable network Showtime. The two-hour specials paid tribute to non-Jews who saved Jews during the Holocaust. Currently in the works for Showtime is *Two Hands That Shook the World*, about the lives of Yitzhak Rabin (the prime minister of Israel from 1974 to 1977) and Yasir Arafat (the Palestinian leader) and the Middle East peace process.

Streisand is also a passionate environmentalist. In 1993 she donated a five-home, 24-acre estate to the Santa Monica Mountains Conservancy to be dedicated as a center for ecological studies. She has been a leading spokesperson and fund-raiser for a variety of other social causes as well, including AIDS research funding. Many of her live concert performances have benefited the various causes she supports.

In 1996, after a four-year break in filmmaking, Streisand released *The Mirror Has Two Faces*, the third film that she produced, directed, and starred in. She plays a hopelessly romantic, although somewhat unattractive, English professor attempting to transform herself into a desirable woman in order to regain the affection of her distant husband, played by Jeff Bridges. The TriStar Pictures romantic comedy received two Oscar nominations in 1997, including one for Streisand as cocomposer of the film's love theme "I Finally Found Someone."

Also in 1997, the "actress who sings," as Barbra refers to herself, released her first album in four years, *Higher Ground*. The work includes the hit single "Tell Him," a duet sung with Celine Dion. *Higher Ground* placed at number one the first week it was released, eventually attaining multiplatinum status and capturing two more Grammy nominations for the multitalented performer of inspirational and love songs.

And once again Barbra Streisand found herself in love, this time with actor James Brolin. He was starring in and serving as executive producer of the syndicated TV series *Pensacola: Wings of Gold*, in which he played a Marine colonel who trains fighter pilots.

On July 2, 1998, the two were wed in a sunset ceremony at her Malibu home. The celebrity crowd of 105 well-wishers included actors Tom Hanks and John Travolta, jazz musician Quincy Jones, and director Steven Spielberg. A rabbi officiated during the ceremony after Streisand's 31-year-old son, Jason Gould, gave the bride away. In exchange for making donations to Barbra's favorite charities, *People* magazine was allowed to cover the elegant affair for its July 20 issue. Meanwhile, outside the compound, 30 walkie-talkie-carrying guards and the blare of heavy-metal music effectively prevented other members of the press from learning about the Streisand-Brolin wedding.

*A scene from the third film that Barbra Streisand directed, produced, and starred in—*The Mirror Has Two Faces. *Streisand also cowrote the love theme "I Finally Found Someone."*

Barbra continues to support Democratic causes. She was one of many Hollywood insiders to support President Bill Clinton in 1998 and 1999 as he struggled with allegations of sexual misconduct and the subsequent impeachment hearings regarding his behavior with White House intern Monica Lewinsky. Among the first to speak out against the impeachment proceedings, Streisand accused the Republican-dominated Congress

Barbra shares an intimate moment with husband James Brolin after he received a star on the Hollywood Walk of Fame, Los Angeles, in August 1998.

of working to undermine the social achievements of the Clinton administration. She continues to support the election campaigns of many Democratic candidates and even endorses some candidates on her website.

Inspired by her relationship with Brolin, in 1999 Streisand released a collection of personal love songs in her album *A Love Like Ours*. A collaborative effort with various producers, songwriters, and arrangers, the work includes a duet with country music superstar Vince Gill, released as the single "If You Ever Leave Me."

In the course of her career, Streisand has made quite an impact in the music industry. According to the Recording Industry Association of America, as of 1999, Barbra Streisand had earned 40 gold and 25 platinum albums, and she was the only female artist ever to have achieved 12 multiplatinum albums. (The soundtrack to

A Star Is Born also went multiplatinum.) She has had number one albums in each of the past four decades. Among her singles releases, she has earned eight gold and five platinum recordings.

Barbra's genius is not easy to define. It is true that her singing voice is remarkably beautiful, but equally remarkable has been her ability to preserve the purity and range of her voice over the decades. Her many other achievements as actress, comedienne, song-writer, director, composer, and filmmaker are certainly the result of her natural talent, but they are also the products of her unrelenting perfectionism. Streisand is never satisfied to simply to take on a demanding new project; instead, she does something over and over again until she gets it exactly right. That passion for perfection is what sets her apart from her colleagues. She is an artist whose imagination brings forth one inspiration after another, but she also has the discipline to craft each new idea with exacting patience. It is ironic that Barbra has so often been criticized for being a perfectionist, for her perfectionism is the hallmark of her professionalism.

Streisand seems destined to remain a star for life. Her talent, drive, and uncanny inventiveness assure her prominent future in the world of music and films both in the United States and abroad. For years, both her fans and her detractors have tried to crack the code of her spellbinding success. But Barbra herself has always understood perfectly why her popularity has lasted so long. She knows she is an emotionally honest performer who keeps her work grounded in the impas-sioned feelings of real human beings. "The people who have kept me a star for thirty-some years have done so because there's a truth to my work and that's what they get," she has said. With courage, diligence, and dramatic intensity, Barbra Streisand will keep telling that truth for years to come.

CHRONOLOGY

1942	Barbara Joan Streisand born on April 24, 1942, in New York City to Emmanuel and Diana Streisand
1959	Graduates from Brooklyn's Erasmus Hall High School
1960	Begins performing at New York City nightclubs; changes spelling of name to *Barbra*
1962	Performs in Broadway show *I Can Get It for You Wholesale*, for which she wins the New York Drama Critics' Circle Award and receives a Tony nomination for Best Supporting Actress; signs recording contract with Columbia Records
1963	Marries fellow actor Elliott Gould on September 13 in Carson City, Nevada; releases first two albums
1964	Stars in Broadway show *Funny Girl*; receives two Grammy Awards for Best Album and for Best Female Vocal Performance for *The Barbra Streisand Album*; five Streisand albums are listed on Billboard's chart of Top 100 Albums
1965	Signs 10-year contract with CBS television; receives two Emmy Awards and Peabody Award for "*My Name Is Barbra*"
1966	Son, Jason Emmanuel Gould, born on December 29
1969	Wins Academy Award for Best Actress for film debut in *Funny Girl*; is also awarded Golden Globe and named Star of the Year by National Association of Theater Owners
1970	Receives Tony Award as Star of the Decade
1971	Divorces Elliott Gould
1972	Establishes her own production company, Barwood Films, and produces *Up the Sandbox*
1977	Receives three Golden Globe Awards for Best Motion Picture, Best Actress, and Best Song ("Evergreen") for *A Star Is Born*; becomes first female composer to win an Academy Award for Best Song
1978	Receives two Grammys for "Evergreen" (Best Female Vocal and Song of the Year)
1981	Receives Grammy for Best Pop Vocal by a Duo (with Barry Gibb) for the song "Guilty"
1983	Becomes first woman to produce, direct, cowrite, and star in a major motion picture with directorial debut of *Yentl*

1984   *Yentl* receives two Golden Globe Awards for Best Director and Best Picture and five Academy Award nominations, although wins only for Best Score

1986   Holds fund-raising concert, One Voice, for Democratic senatorial candidates

1987   Receives Best Pop Female Vocal Grammy Award for *The Broadway Album*

1991   Directs and stars in *The Prince of Tides*, the first motion picture directed by its female star to receive, in 1992, a Best Director nomination from the Directors Guild of America; the film also receives seven Academy Award nominations

1992   Receives Living Legend Grammy Award

1993   Gives 24-acre estate to the Santa Monica Mountains Conservancy; 50th album, *Back to Broadway*, released and appears on *Billboard*'s chart at number one

1994   Holds 12-stop concert tour, which provides basis of HBO special entitled "Barbra: The Concert"

1995   Wins two Emmys and the Peabody Award for "Barbra: The Concert"; is awarded Grammy Award for Lifetime Achievement

1997   Performs duet with Celine Dion on Grammy-nominated hit single "Tell Him"; nominated for Academy Award as cocomposer of "I Finally Found Someone," from the 1996 film *The Mirror Has Two Faces*; album *Higher Ground* becomes number one the first week after its release

1998   Marries television actor James Brolin

1999   New Year's Eve show at Las Vegas's MGM Grand Hotel generates biggest U.S. box office gross to date for a single performance: $14.7 million

2000   Receives the Cecil B. DeMille Award for "outstanding contribution to the entertainment field" at the 57th Annual Golden Globe Awards; kicks off concert tour in Australia

DISCOGRAPHY

I Can Get It for You Wholesale, 1962

Pins and Needles, 1962

The Barbra Streisand Album, 1963

The Second Barbra Streisand Album, 1963

Barbra Streisand/The Third Album, 1964

Funny Girl (Broadway musical), 1964

People, 1964

My Name Is Barbra, 1965

My Name Is Barbra Two, 1965

Color Me Barbra, 1966

Je M'Appelle Barbra, 1966

A Christmas Album, 1967

Simply Streisand, 1967

Funny Girl (movie soundtrack), 1968

A Happening in Central Park, 1968

Barbra Streisand's Greatest Hits, 1969

Hello, Dolly! 1969

What About Today? 1969

On a Clear Day You Can See Forever, 1970

The Owl and the Pussycat, 1970

Barbra Joan Streisand, 1971

Stoney End, 1971

Live Concert at the Forum, 1972

Barbra Streisand . . . and Other Musical Instruments, 1973

ButterFly, 1974

The Way We Were, 1974

Funny Lady, 1975

Lazy Afternoon, 1975

Classical Barbra, 1976

A Star Is Born, 1976

Streisand Superman, 1977

Barbra Streisand's Greatest Hits, Volume 2, 1978

Songbird, 1978

The Main Event, 1979

Wet, 1979

Guilty, 1980

Memories, 1981

Yentl, 1983

Emotion, 1984

The Broadway Album, 1985

Nuts, 1987

One Voice, 1987

Till I Loved You, 1988

A Collection/Greatest Hits . . . and More, 1989

Just for the Record, 1991

The Prince of Tides, 1991

Back to Broadway, 1993

Barbra: The Concert, 1994

Higher Ground, 1996

The Mirror Has Two Faces, 1996

A Love Like Ours, 1999

FILM, TELEVISION, AND STAGE APPEARANCES

FILMS

Funny Girl, 1968

Hello Dolly! 1969

On a Clear Day You Can See Forever, 1970

The Owl and the Pussycat, 1970

Up the Sandbox, 1972

What's Up Doc? 1972

The Way We Were, 1973

For Pete's Sake, 1974

Funny Lady, 1975

A Star Is Born, 1976 (executive producer, star)

The Main Event, 1979 (producer, star)

All Night Long, 1981

Yentl, 1983 (director, producer, star, cowriter)

Nuts, 1987

The Prince of Tides, 1991 (director, producer, star)

The Mirror Has Two Faces, 1996 (director, producer, star)

TELEVISION SPECIALS

"My Name Is Barbra," April, 28, 1965

"Color Me Barbra," March 30, 1966

"The Belle of 14th Street," October 11, 1967

"Barbra Streisand: A Happening in Central Park," September 15, 1968

"Barbra Streisand . . . and Other Musical Instruments," November 2, 1973

"The Stars Salute Israel at 30," May 8, 1978

"Putting It Together—The Making of the Broadway Album," January 11, 1986

"Barbra Streisand: One Voice," December 27, 1986

"Barbra Streisand: The Tour of the Century," April 20, 1994

"Barbra: The Concert," August 21, 1994

FILM, TELEVISION, AND STAGE APPEARANCES

TELEVISION MOVIES

Serving in Silence: The Margarethe Cammermeyer Story, 1995 (executive producer)

Rescuers: Stories of Courage—Two Women, 1997 (executive producer)

The Long Island Incident, TV movie, 1998 (executive producer)

Rescuers: Stories of Courage—Two Couples, 1998 (executive producer)

STAGE APPEARANCES

Another Evening with Harry Stoones, 1961 Gramercy Arts Theatre

I Can Get It for You Wholesale, 1962 Shubert Theatre

Funny Girl, 1964 Winter Garden Theatre

Funny Girl, 1966 Wales Theatre, London

FURTHER READING

Bly, Nellie. *Barbra Streisand: The Untold Story*. New York: Pinnacle Books, 1994.

Cunningham, Ernest W. *The Ultimate Barbra*. Los Angeles, Calif.: Renaissance Books, 1998.

Edwards, Anne. *Streisand: A Biography*. Boston, Mass.: Little, Brown, and Co., 1997.

Riese, Randall. *Her Name Is Barbra*. New York: Birch Lane, 1993.

Ruhlmann, William. *Barbra Streisand*. Stamford, Conn.: Longmeadow Press, 1995.

Spada, James. *Streisand: Her Life*. New York: Crown, 1995.

———. *Streisand: The Woman and the Legend*. New York: Doubleday, 1981.

Vare, Ethlie Ann, ed. *Diva: Barbra Streisand and the Making of a Superstar*. New York: Boulevard Books, 1996.

Waldman, Allison J. *The Barbra Streisand Scrapbook*. New York: Citadel, 1995.

WEBSITES

The Official Barbra Streisand Site
http://www.barbrastreisand.com/

Barbra Streisand News
http://www.barbra-streisand.com/

The Barbra Streisand Music Guide
http://www.bjsmusic.com/

INDEX

PICTURE CREDITS

Rita Pappas received her B.A. in English from Douglass College, New Jersey, and her M.A. in Italian from Rutgers University, New Jersey. A widely published poet, she lives in Princeton, New Jersey, where she works for the Educational Testing Service.

Matina S. Horner was president of Radcliffe College and associate professor of psychology and social relations at Harvard University. She is best known for her studies of women's motivation, achievement, and personality development. Dr. Horner has served on several national boards and advisory councils, including those of the National Science Foundation, Time Inc., and the Women's Research and Education Institute. She earned her B.A. from Bryn Mawr College and her Ph.D. from the University of Michigan, and holds honorary degrees from many colleges and universities, including Mount Holyoke, Smith, Tufts, and the University of Pennsylvania.